'A really useful and invaluable toolki

'An essential read for both the season
alike. Packed with practical exercises, it explores the key elements that
go into creating physical-theatre performance. At the same time,
it places these techniques within the wider historical context of theatre
development. As a director, this book has made me rethink my use of
the theatrical space, the physical relationship between actors, and how
I tell stories.' *Michael O'Hara, Head of Learning and Participation at
Birmingham Rep*

'One of the most comprehensive and easy-to-use guides to collaborative
physical-theatre practice. Drawing on a wide range of training practices
and approaches, it offers the reader a way to understand how theatre
exercises relate to the learning of skills and how those skills are part of a
broader picture of the development of physical theatre in the last two
decades.' *Professor Mark Evans, Professor of Theatre Training and
Education, Coventry University*

'A splendid and often groundbreaking work, we feel as if we have been
given the tangible experience of doing; we emerge from the journey with
a visceral sense of the transformational possibilities within and between
human bodies. *Through the Body* begins as a deceptively plain-spoken
primer on physical theatre, invaluable for any performing artist seeking
greater breadth of expression, historical understanding, and
philosophical inspiration. However, the book ventures beyond the
performer and into ensemble work, and the final two chapters represent
an excellent starting point for those interested in this often nebulous
and uniquely challenging process.' *Richard Stockton Rand, Professor of
Theatre, Purdue University, Indiana*

'*Through the Body* was a profound influence on me as an emerging
researcher, educator and practitioner of devised and physical theatre. It
distilled both intellectual and embodied understanding of various
physical-theatre traditions into an accessible and user-friendly volume.
Dymphna Callery has now turned her attention to activating the visual
and physical dimensions of playtexts, in a volume that I have no doubt
will have as significant an influence on students, practitioners and
researchers as the first.' *Dr Alex Mermikides, Senior Lecturer in Drama,
Kingston University*

Dymphna Callery

Dymphna Callery was a librarian before discovering drama as an undergraduate at Sheffield University. Her theatre credits include Ibsen's *A Doll's House* and Edna O'Brien's *Virginia*, as well as writing stage adaptations of *Thérèse Raquin* and *Women in Love*. She has a masters degree in Writing Studies, and her poetry collection *What She Said and What She Did* was published in 1996.

She has taught drama and writing at Liverpool John Moores University and the University of Wolverhampton, and conducted workshops in Britain and abroad, in addition to working on community-arts projects. She has served on the boards of Foursight Theatre, Kaos Theatre and Gazebo Theatre-in-Education.

Numerous workshops with a variety of physical-theatre practitioners fed her research for *Through the Body: A Practical Guide to Physical Theatre*, her first book, published by Nick Hern Books in 2001, and translated into Korean in 2014.

Dymphna Callery
The Active Text

*Unlocking Plays Through
Physical Theatre*

NICK HERN BOOKS
London
www.nickhernbooks.co.uk

A Nick Hern Book

The Active Text
First published in Great Britain in 2015
by Nick Hern Books Limited
The Glasshouse, 49a Goldhawk Road, London W12 8QP

Cover design by Christopher Clegg

Designed and typeset by Nick Hern Books, London
Printed and bound in Great Britain by
Ashford Colour Press, Gosport, Hampshire

A CIP catalogue record for this book
is available from the British Library

ISBN 978 1 84842 127 1

Contents

Foreword

One of the most influential modern teachers of theatre, Jacques Lecoq, says that in theatre as well as in life, *tout bouge* ('everything moves').[1] He doesn't just mean obvious, physical movement, but suggests a deeper level of cycles, processes, causes and effects – *movement* – which underpins and permeates the world around us and how it should appear on stage. It is Lecoq's idea, that everything causes or is subject to movement – in its most profound definition and whether discernible to the eye or not – which drives *The Active Text*. What sits underneath, around, filters through and animates a text is explored throughout the book. This is anything but a literary approach, which all too often encourages performers to sit around a table and discuss a text, but, to follow Lecoq, is instead a call to investigate a play up on our feet, finding out what makes it *move*.

Structured in eight sections and referring to some thirteen plays, we are invited to move through aspects such as considering an audience, understanding situations and the structure of plays, and how characters can be created and function. Always with an eye to an ultimate performance, the book also considers space and the musicality of language, stage directions and the importance of silence. It is peppered throughout with useful quotations from diverse practitioners, placing the work in a wider context of theatre practices, whilst rejecting convenient labels of genre, style or traditions. Full of fresh ideas, it leads the reader through approaches stage by stage, augmenting established theatre practice and the work of many writers, performers and directors. There are plenty of notes and a bibliography to help readers follow up further lines of enquiry. You can dip in and out as needed, though I'd recommend reading cover to cover: each section is a progression from the last and, overall, offers a complete approach to working on a play, something that the author insists is so much more than just a script. She maintains that a text itself is *active*: the words on the page of a playscript are the active representation of a complex world. A play is also made of language that works actively. We are asked to be active in our approach to working on text, ultimately asking our audiences to become actively involved too.

All of this is fuelled by the author's own experience and ability to pull diverse approaches together in a joined-up, meaningful way. Rather than a handbook, each section demonstrates an acute sense of how a play works with rich and insightful discussion around the more hands-on work. Straightforward and clear in its style, it is suitable for actors and students, directors and teachers. And one of the ways that *The Active Text* is especially empowering to its readers is that it enables groups working without a leader or 'outside eye' to get to grips with a play in new and imaginative ways, working holistically and often as an ensemble.

The author is careful to say that *The Active Text* is not just an extension of her previous book, *Through the Body*. Like many people working and teaching in the theatre, I have often turned to that book for advice, inspiration and, to be honest, when I've been just plain stuck. And, like that book, *The Active Text* is full of useful, immediate and creative approaches to use in rehearsal and workshops of plays. Dick McCaw, writing in the Foreword to *Through the Body*, warns us that exercises

> aren't a *recipe* for success, rather they are open structures by means of which we can make psycho-physical connections within ourselves. They are possible pathways though our mental and physical structure which can lead toward a mental and emotional experience.[2]

The Active Text attempts to suggest approaches that bring together mind and body and how an actor thus encounters the playtext with their *whole* self. Yes, no one can offer easy recipes for success, but what this book does do is to offer a set of clearly thought-through approaches which provide anyone working practically on a play a series of logical, clearly beneficial and developmental stages of investigation.

I know that Dymphna is a highly creative teacher, offering students challenges drawn from her eclectic experience, distilled through her role as (to return to Lecoq) a 'zero point'.[3] Many of us work in, and are increasingly products of, education systems driven by targets and the learning of neat packages of information. All too often, this can ultimately lead to thin knowledge. Added to this is the tradition, especially in the university sector, of logocentrism. Thankfully, much of the rise in theatre studies in higher education values other types of *knowledges*: those of creativity, the sensibility of the body, group work and instinct. As this book advocates, there needs to be a healthy balance between analysis, intellectual curiosity and time for, as Section 2 puts it, 'serious play'. Not everything is measurably knowable through books and through writing down. I hope too that the school system can hold on to such values. And in our theatre work, short-term, target-driven ('getting the show on') practice is ultimately to cheat our audiences. This book offers the chance to take responsibility, to engage in a deeper knowledge that embraces process, finding out, and understanding the substance of the play through the intelligence of our more creative selves.

Adam J. Ledger
University of Birmingham, March 2014

Introduction

This book is rooted in uncovering visual dimensions and physical embodiment for theatre-makers working with a scripted play. Games, exercises and ideas for creative investigations are drawn both from those who use them in the rehearsal room and from my own work with student actors and directors. My approach is eclectic, raiding sources from playwrights as well as theatre-makers – directors, practitioners and actors – who have written about or been interviewed about their crafting and rehearsal practices, with references largely confined to them rather than those who theorise about theatre and performance.[4] A continual process of practical exploration and experimentation leads to discoveries about a play rather than arriving at interpretation through round-the-table analysis and discussion. Work is orientated to activating signifying systems of the stage where the spoken word takes equal place with other elements. Critical viewing and feedback through showing and sharing become cornerstones of praxis. I advocate embracing an open stage/spectator relationship in rehearsals to promote an awareness of the eventual presence of the audience, one which fuels the players' ability to connect with them.

To truly understand a play is to discover it through embodiment. And that happens in the throes of exploring it practically rather than round a table or sat at a desk. A play is a complex web of interwoven threads; there are various logics at work in its construction, and these need to be accessed in order to fuel practical realisation. Events and themes in the plotting, characters and dialogue are entwined like threads in a rug. In the craft of weaving, needles are in constant motion to knit coloured threads together, and the design emerges only once the rug comes off the loom. Uncovering the internal dynamics of a play, unravelling its threads and how these are knitted together, yields insights: its image structure becomes manifest when the language of performance embedded in its fabric is unearthed.

A text is always active in performance, always moving, vibrating, transmitting once it is embodied by players. During a performance, spectators may be affected by the agility of the movement, sonorities in actors' voices, moments where a player seems to offer something indefinable in response to events or to another player, because everything occurring on stage transmits dynamic and kinaesthetic signals. We accept this in dance. *The Active Text* views theatre as having the idea of dance at its centre. It offers a gestural approach to working with a scripted play: theatre is a game, actors are players, texts are re-inscribed through bodies in space.

Because we meet a play through words on a page there's a temptation to begin work by reading through, or walking through with script in hand, based on the idea that the words will be fleshed out by action and ges-

'I never start with a readthrough. For the first few days I do everything but the text!'[5]

Declan Donnellan

ture in order to bring the play to life. This is essentially a literary approach where activity is viewed as something ascertained through discussion, understanding is generated through reason, and 'action' becomes additional to the spoken word. A playscript may consist predominantly of dialogue, and it is dialogue that appears to hold it together. But ask yourself, once you've seen a play, what it was about? You are likely to answer by saying what *happens* in the play, because dialogue is, as Rib Davies reminds would-be playwrights, 'utterly entwined with... the characterisation, the plot, the action, the structure, the visual effects, the music'.[6]

'We are,' says the director Mike Alfreds, 'in search of deep structures that aren't necessarily apparent from a linear reading [and] what we find will lead us to matters of theme and form'.[7] So we need to understand how the play functions. Working with a play means breathing life not only into the words but the text as a whole. The fuller an understanding of the text, the richer the acting. The word 'text' comes from the Latin *'texere'*, which means texture in association with weaving, and it is the interweaving of all the various elements of theatre that creates the play for an audience. Theatre isn't just about what we see and hear, and there are various components at work of which an unfolding narrative is just one. Theatre with the idea of dance at its centre is vital and physical for both performers and their audiences. There is a sensory nature to live theatre; it feels *alive*. Creating theatre to provoke sensorial effects demands invoking body and imagination to transform the players and transport the onlookers. To do this, it's necessary to separate out the parts, rather like a mechanic taking apart an engine, before reassembling it. For Eugenio Barba, 'dramaturgy [is] similar to "anatomy"'... a practical way of working not only on the organism in its totality, but on its different organs and layers'.[8] He talks of three levels that operate as layers, inseparable in performance yet distinct in the making: organic, narrative and evocative. The organic focuses on the actors' somatic and vocal work and how these affect spectators at a sensorial level; narrative dramaturgy concerns itself with the generation of meaning; and evocative dramaturgy 'distils or captures the performance's unintentional and concealed meanings, specific for each spectator'.[9] For a play to come alive in performance, image, gesture, and words can be worked on separately in the rehearsal process before integrating them into the whole.

'The text becomes a score of physical actions inspired by and attached to impulses.'[10]

John Harrop

Too many preconceptions before rehearsals can place a play in a straitjacket, denying the growth of mutual understanding through practice. The same seriously playful process applied in devising work is applied in this book to exploring a text. Like devising, this is a collaborative approach to experimenting through improvisation, finding and testing out what works theatrically and what doesn't work via physical engagement and interaction. So although *The Active Text* is not strictly speaking a 'sequel' to my earlier book *Through the Body: A Practical Guide to Physical Theatre*, for those familiar with that book there is an obvious correlation. Jacques Lecoq appears regularly as a point of reference and inspiration, together with the voices of other practitioners who reiterate a similar concern with the actor's body, including the director Mike Alfreds who believes in the body 'as a means of reaching the imagination and releasing spontaneous truth'.[11] And it is Joan Littlewood, whom writer and director Stella Duffy calls the 'mother of modern British theatre', who has informed much of the thinking behind this book.[12] Her search for theatrical vitality in the latter half of the twentieth century led to highly imaginative staging solutions arrived at through collaborative work, using improvisatory and devising techniques rooted in active bodies.

There is no single way to produce a play. Stage and performance conventions of every age mean any new production of the same play discovers different meanings, and perhaps reveals new dimensions. Every so often theatre seems to reinvent itself; styles come and go as playwrights and practitioners respond to developments in society, culture, technology and art. The history of Western theatre is strewn with challenges to supposed authorities of style and form, whether in the kinds of plays written or kinds of performance created, as well as the styles of acting. My aim is not to come up with a new theory or method but to invigorate the rehearsal process with ideas and suggestions to combine the somatic with the semantic. What works for one play might not work for another. In this sense devising offers a useful model.

There are many excellent and inspirational books on acting and directing; the majority address the individual rather than a company of players. In this book the work is designed predominantly with a group in mind rather than an individual actor or director.

'In an ensemble, actors are part of the interpretative decision-making and they have to create things as a team.'[13]

Annabel Arden

Physical explorations help players communicate effectively with each other and with an audience who 'read with their eyes' to a large extent. Working through the body enables players to gain a fuller realisation of the text as they experience every aspect of it, from mapping its structure to playing with imagery and digging into the words. Storytelling techniques and strategies for creating stage pictures are offered that may challenge assumptions about particular plays or preconceived ideas about directing, acting and rehearsing a play. Employing playful processes, physical and imaginative improvisation creates a stripped-down aesthetic suited to workshop or studio performance, as well as fuelling production in professional contexts.

While it is beyond the parameters of this book to engage with design, if you intend to produce a performance with people responsible for designing set, costume, lighting, sound or digital technology, whether site-specifically or in a theatre, they should belong to the ensemble and be working alongside the company in rehearsals. The work suggested here does not depend on expensive production values or scenographic elements, rather it acquaints players with the concept of establishing scenic environments through image and sound. While the environment of a play's story needs to give characters' actions a distinct context, creating worlds can happen without piling scenery on stage. Necessary furniture can be substituted; a few blocks used imaginatively can represent a great deal even for a play assumed to be 'naturalistic'.

Labels are not always helpful in describing theatrical styles although we use them conversationally as a kind of shorthand, as for example 'naturalistic' and 'realistic', and some companies and practitioners become attached to certain labels by virtue of the way they are described by critics and academics. 'Physical theatre' is a case in point. The term 'physical theatre' has been hotly debated: theatre artists and companies often resent the label while academics and critics debate its provenance and application. Playwright and director Alan Ayckbourn complains that 'It suggests that somewhere there is a non-physical theatre. What theatre isn't or shouldn't be to some extent physical?'[14] Frantic Assembly's co-directors, who choreograph like dancers but were not trained as dancers, work with scripted texts and call their productions 'shows', grumble that 'Physical theatre is actually quite a frustrating phrase as it barely manages to describe what we do never mind the wide range of styles and influences that are clustered under its banner.'[15]

'All theatre is visual. Not all theatre is verbal.'[16]

Mike Alfreds

As shorthand, 'physical theatre' served (and perhaps still serves) a valuable purpose in acknowledging a visually resonant style of theatre created by a variety of spirited ensemble companies towards the end of the twentieth century: theatre celebrating its difference as an art form from film and television; theatre rediscovering storytelling through action; a theatre combining movement, music, design (including digital media) and text, in an integrated whole, underpinned by the potency of the language of the body. Their work continues to mature as well as influence the next generation of writers, directors and performers, who have begun forging new ways of making theatre and performance, making an impact on the way theatre is created, staged, received, studied and taught. Theatre ecology in the twenty-first century is already exceptionally mixed; despite the pervasive hangover of conventional methodologies and practices in some sectors, theatre has shown itself capable of much more than presenting a convincing slice of life. And twenty-first century audiences have a sophisticated acquaintance with visual aesthetics from exposure to cinema, television, cartoons, digital media and the visual arts. Our narrative vocabulary has reached new heights via rock concerts, pop videos, commercials and video games, so we are open not only to new ways of seeing but to new ways of storytelling.

As boundaries between traditional forms and styles of performance blur, it is no surprise that exciting physical and visual theatre is increasingly tangible in productions of scripted plays. But no discussion of physical theatre should ignore Jacques Lecoq, whose ideas permeate this book. His book is published in English as *The Moving Body* but was originally published in his native French as *Le Corps Poetique* – i.e. 'the poetic body'. Interestingly, Lecoq never used the term 'physical theatre', simply 'theatre'. Rather than viewing the body as the actor's instrument, for Lecoq the body is both instrument and player, where creativity, intuition, imagination and feeling coalesce. Together with two key personnel associated with his Paris school, Philippe Gaulier and Monika Pagneux, his impact has been particularly noticeable as part of a trend in Britain for physically and visually orientated theatre, and graduates and companies formed by Lecoq graduates appear on the touring circuit not only in Britain but across the globe.[17]

However, companies who are often labelled 'physical theatre' frequently sport directors who did not attend Lecoq's school: Kneehigh and Frantic Assembly

> *'The body is where you begin in the rehearsal room.'*[18]
>
> Simon McBurney

are just two examples. Kneehigh's Artistic Director Emma Rice trained as an actor and spent some time with the Polish company Gardzienice, who draw on folk and storytelling in vibrant physical/visual/musical ways. Scott Graham and Steven Hoggett, joint artistic founders of Frantic Assembly,[19] studied English Literature in Swansea when they were blown away by a workshop with Volcano Theatre and set out to emulate them; subsequently the dance films of David Hinton for DV8 exerted a significant influence and they have said they find film more inspirational than theatre. Declan Donnellan of Cheek by Jowl and Mike Alfreds, who set up Shared Experience, are two directors whose words and advice feature often in this book, and neither has trained with Lecoq.

While movement is a primary element in theatre, physicality has to earn its place when serving a piece. Explosive or high-octane expression excites an audience just as it does in circus or dance; yet physicality can also be nuanced and subtle, with stillness and minimal movement creating a searing intensity. Both can exist within the same performance, and both can offer an audience the visceral thrill that makes theatre so potently alive. Cheek by Jowl, Kneehigh, Frantic Assembly and Complicite are companies who exemplify this, presenting work where the spoken word is meshed with physical, visual and musical languages. Theirs is a theatre that acknowledges craftsmanship, passion and imagination, forged in collaborative and compositional ways with physically based improvisation as the bedrock, whether they are working on adapting a story, developing an original piece or working on a play. They enter the text through the body with devising methodologies as the seedbed of interpretation.

'The best achievements of a good ensemble can far outstrip any virtuoso display an actor might pull off alone.'[20]

Harriet Walter

A key attribute of these companies is the notion of an actor-centred approach, with members who relish the creative charge of working collectively – not always purely as devisers since many are equally keen on working with texts. For them, the challenge of working as equal partners is not only hugely appealing but the *only* way to make theatre. And, of course, that is not exclusive to the younger generation of theatre-makers. Littlewood, Brecht and Brook are recognised as hugely influential beyond the post-war period, and for all of them collaborative work with actors is at the centre of the process.

Many critics and commentators struggle with the idea and practice of collaboration. A preference persists for assigning artistic ownership by naming an individual as responsible for a piece of theatre. Although much is made of the ethos of collaborative work in devising, when it comes to text work a prevailing notion that hierarchical principles govern a rehearsal process seems to kick in, with the idea of the director as the 'visionary' rather like some orchestral conductors who are regarded as 'maestro'. Yet time and again companies where the director is admired and fêted are those whose working practices are rooted in genuine collaboration.

No one has articulated the ethos of collaboration better than Joan Littlewood in her 'Goodbye Note' of 1961:

> I do not believe in the supremacy of the director, designer, actor or even of the writer. It is through collaboration that this knockabout art of theatre survives and kicks. It was true of The Globe, The Curtain, The Crown... No one mind or imagination can foresee what a play will become until all the physical and intellectual stimuli, which are crystallised in the poetry of the author, have been understood by a company, and then tried out in terms of mime, discussion, and the precise music of grammar: words and movement allied and integrated.[21]

And it is her philosophy which governs the idea behind and the ideas within this book.

Littlewood's way of working through improvisation and games served to sketch in the action in broad strokes before filling in the detail. While her approach owed much to Stanislavsky, with actors breaking down a play into units and objectives, her stagecraft had a radical edge, more attuned to the ideas of Meyerhold or Copeau and drawing on *commedia dell'arte* and Chinese principles in opening out the relationship between the stage and spectator. She was not a devotee of naturalistic staging techniques, preferring to use whatever worked in matters of style. And if something didn't work she had no compunction about scrapping it and starting again. Games and structured improvisation as routes to ensemble-building and approaching a text were key principles. She used a range of physical games and exercises as creative catalysts to open up the text.

Littlewood's notion of playful improvisation as the major approach to working with, and developing an interpretation of, a scripted text underpins this book. The idea of improvisation-

> *Games and exercises 'develop initiative, excite curiosity, exercise the imagination.'*[22]
>
> Joan Littlewood

as-exploration is not new. Over a century ago, Stanislavsky realised improvisation gave actors a quicker and more vital access to experiencing a play than could be achieved through intellectual discussion. Theatre practitioners and directors who work collaboratively advocate harnessing the imagination, initiative, intuition and intelligence of everyone involved. The principle is 'don't talk, just do'.

There are thirteen plays referred to in the course of this book, drawn largely from the so-called classical repertoire and those featured regularly on higher education and school syllabi. They are: Sophocles's *Antigone*; Shakespeare's *A Midsummer Night's Dream, Macbeth* and *Hamlet*; Georg Büchner's *Woyzeck*; Oscar Wilde's *The Importance of Being Earnest*; Bertolt Brecht's *Mother Courage and Her Children*; Samuel Beckett's *Waiting for Godot*; Arthur Miller's *A View from the Bridge*; Edward Bond's *Saved*; Steven Berkoff's *Greek*; Caryl Churchill's *Top Girls*; Sarah Kane's *Blasted*. Given my potential readership, I anticipate that most will be familiar with these plays as actors and directors, teachers and students of theatre. As examples of plays that have stood the test of time, they examine what we think and feel about ourselves; the human condition doesn't change very much and these plays hang on in the repertoire and remain classic texts for study because they still have something to offer.[23] And they are plays that alter with every ensemble, who discover new nuances, new ideas, new possibilities latent in the scripts as they make them active for performance. The plays and editions used are listed separately in the bibliography.

What follows is designed to promote openness and simplicity, intensity in atmosphere, absolute focus and commitment from every player, whether they end up as the protagonist or a member of the chorus. It requires generosity of spirit. It is not intended as a linear 'method', although some logic exists in the order in which sections are presented. Feel free to dip in and out if that suits.

Section 1: Plays and Audiences looks at how meaning(s) operate through genre, theme, structure, suspense and time, and the impact of these on an audience during performance. The ways in which the audience offer their attention, curiosity and empathy, informs this and is central to ensuing sections.

Section 2: Serious Play establishes the fundamental importance of play as an essential training and rehearsal tool, opening doors to improvisatory states and opening up choices and possibilities for analysis and interpretation of scripted plays.

Section 3: Mapping a Play starts with animating and transforming space as an essential basis for working on stage as a precursor to discovering the topography of a play. It contains exercises to illustrate the nature of dramatic composition, providing routes for connecting players to the overall shape and pattern and a play's flow.

Section 4: Charting Journeys offers starting points for bringing characters alive through their connections to the design of the play, their route through it and the situations they face. Collective engagement as well as personal investment from players undergirds the practice.

Section 5: Workshopping Scenes assumes acquaintance with the previous two sections with work orientated to the detail of individual scenes. The emphasis is on expressing actions with visual resonance, with suggestions relating to scoring and framing these.

Section 6: Inside the Words builds on the understanding gained, moving on to tackle the words to be spoken as an active force, exploring their sonic, rhythmic, dynamic and semantic values.

Section 7: Around the Words gets to grips with the words that speak without being uttered, activating stage directions, objects, locations and silence to unpeel the image structure of a play and its emotional and metaphorical dimensions.

Section 8: Shaping and Pacing incorporates work on music as a shaping device, tension states and the importance of rhythm and pace in making the maximum impact on the audience.

Acknowledgements

Thanks are due to Peter Cann for ongoing conversations throughout the development of this book, and especially to Jane Hartley for her input through conversations and critical readings of early drafts. I am indebted to colleagues in the Drama Department at the University of Wolverhampton for their interest and support for this book, and to students there who have been wonderful collaborators over the past decade or so. Thanks are also due to friends and family who have accompanied me on many theatre trips and offered valuable insights; they have informed my thinking about and appreciation of theatre in all its myriad forms. The editorial steer of Nick Hern has been invaluable, and his enthusiasm and critical comments have spurred me on in the latter stages of writing. Any errors are my own. Finally, very many thanks to my close relatives and friends for their understanding when I was chained to my computer and missing from their company.

The author and publisher gratefully acknowledge permission to quote extracts from the following: *Top Girls* by Caryl Churchill, *Saved* by Edward Bond, and *Blasted* by Sarah Kane, all published by Bloomsbury Methuen Drama, reproduced by permission of Bloomsbury Publishing Plc. *Waiting for Godot* by Samuel Beckett, and *Greek* by Steven Berkoff in *Collected Plays: Volume 1*, both published by Faber and Faber Ltd, and reproduced by permission of Faber and Faber Ltd. *Antigone* by Sophocles, translated and introduced by Marianne McDonald, *Blue Heart* by Caryl Churchill, *The Importance of Being Earnest* by Oscar Wilde, introduced by Dan Rebellato, and *Woyzeck* by Georg Büchner, translated and introduced by Gregory Motton, all published by Nick Hern Books Ltd. *A View from the Bridge* by Arthur Miller, published by Penguin Books, reproduced by permission of The Wylie Agency. Every effort has been made to trace copyright holders, but if any have been inadvertently overlooked, the publisher will be pleased to make the necessary arrangements at the first opportunity.

Section 1

Plays and Audiences

Plays and Audiences

It's all too easy to forget about the audience, especially in workshop or practical-study contexts. Yet in performance, a play takes place in the minds of the audience.

The word audience derives from the Latin *audientia*, which means a 'hearing' and implies listening. In French and modern Latin countries the word for the audience is like our word 'spectator', which may go some way to explaining the oft-remarked variance between those countries attuned to visual aspects of theatre and the British tradition, more formally concerned with words. Considering the audience as 'spectators' forces a consideration of them as onlookers, watching actively as in sport. Like English speakers, the French distinguish between the individual and the collective in theatre audiences: the spectator is the grammatically singular *un spectateur*, while the audience is frequently described by the collective noun *l'assistance*, a word whose secondary meaning – i.e. 'helping' – indicates the presence of the audience as more than simply listening and watching. Emma Rice, Artistic Director of Kneehigh theatre company, likes to call the audience 'accomplices', capturing her notion of them as participants in theatre as a storytelling event.

> '*Everything should be about making that connection between the actor and the audience – that's what theatre should be about.*'[24]
>
> Mark Rylance

The idea of the audience as a homogenous body has been tainted to some extent by the realisation that a collection of individual spectators do not necessarily share the same thoughts and responses. Each of us comes with a set of personal and cultural circumstances, sociopolitical views, outlooks on life that will affect our response to the action on stage. However, to a certain extent, spectators accept that for the duration of the performance they are in a similar boat and have shared expectations of the 'experience' they will have together.

Being transported to a new reality on stage is central to the magic and richness of theatre. Part of the experience for us as individuals is to be taken deep into our selves; what we witness on stage activates reflection on our own lives, our own histories and circumstances, striking chords or challenging preconceptions of our knowledge and experience of the world. Theatre activates our inner world: the border between that hinterland of mind and memory loosens, and we tap into our own playfulness, connecting with the ideas transmitted from the stage. While we might connect with aspects of a performance individually, we don't surrender our personal response but add a collective one. If you go to theatre on your own, something happens in the process of responding with those around you. You react individually, yet also respond as a member of the collective. There is something akin to a congregational power in that shared experience of being gathered together with strangers and becoming 'the audience', perhaps because a certain amount of reassurance comes from the presence of others. While individuals may see the play from different perspectives, there is simultaneity in sharing the experience with others at the same time. Whatever an academic analysis of differential audience responses, at the time of the performance we see ourselves in some respect as an entity and are treated by the actors as such – they perceive us as one.

'A performance is more absorbed than understood.'[25]

John Harrop

In this sense we respond instinctively and feed off one another in creating atmosphere and responding. It's most obvious when laughter ripples through our bodies: we tend to laugh louder and longer when surrounded by others laughing, so the collective nature of being a group of spectators becomes audible, and thereby more tangible. Our laughter rewards those on stage, rising up like a wave when everyone imagines or recognises the same thing at the same time and sees the funny side or gets the joke. A quality of intense silence accompanying the profound or deeply tragic is similarly transmitted back to the stage. It's a current of exchange reminiscent of a radio frequency, an invisible but palpable channel of communication: 'It doesn't have to be comedy. It can be silence in the audience. It can be weeping. It can be something as simple as your awareness of the way that an audience is paying attention,' says Simon McBurney.[26] When this two-way transmission between stage and spectator is at its height, a curious blurring of our individual subjective response and the collective one occurs. There is, in such special moments, no border between us. We share the moment. Something indefinable flows, however fleetingly.

'When the audience's imagination and the actors' imagination are perfectly joined something is born between them.'[27]

Declan Donnellan

We tend to assume such moments happen only in major theatre productions with star actors. They can also happen in rehearsals with a group of players presenting a scene to their peers, and although such telling moments may not happen often, the surge of understanding they create when they do is priceless. Stanislavsky worked with his actors as audience, and the first lesson on action in *An Actor Prepares* is to simply sit on the stage, not acting 'being purposeless' but actually just sitting, being purposeless but watchable. Lecoq is well known for his *auto-cours* method, whereby students perform their scenarios to test their work in front of others. Both replicated the stage/spectator relationship as a strategy to enrich the actors' understanding of how an audience interpret and invest meaning. Presenting work to others teaches players to work with the gaze of spectators, to recognise how the placing of people and objects, the space between them, the looks and attitudes, beats around words, tones of delivery, all configure to project meaning, shared understanding, and possibly move an audience emotionally. Many of the exercises and suggestions in this book rely on the assumption that those using this book will manage rehearsals in this way, not least because enormous amounts can be gained through observing others testing out ideas.

For Brecht, theatre embraced two art forms: acting and spectating, and for Meyerhold the audience was the 'fourth creator' (the other three being the actor, the writer and the director). Both acknowledged the audience as avid spectators actively searching out connections and meanings, co-narrating a play, as they piece together incidents, figuring out who does what to whom and interpreting everything the actors do, even when they do nothing, as *actions*. 'Everything that the actor does on stage, even if he is doing nothing, is interpreted by the spectator as action,'[29] actions that relate to what has happened, is happening or might happen, and re-evaluating those actions in relation to whatever else they glean as the play progresses. From this perspective, rehearsals become a process of sorting out pieces of a jigsaw to give the audience the pleasure of completing the whole picture.

> *'I believe in the intelligence of the audience, I believe that the audience wants to create.'*[28]
>
> Robert Lepage

> *'The core emotional impact of dramatic storytelling lies in anticipation.'*[30]
>
> Steve Waters

A theatre audience is loaded with anticipation even before the play begins, armed with expectation, experience and assumptions. Peter Hall describes audiences as 'quick-witted', their anticipation sparking alacrity in seizing on allusions, suggestions, an echo, a pattern. As we recognise conventions in a storyline, in the characters, or aesthetics, we start to guess at possible outcomes. Frantic Assembly's co-directors keep in mind that 'a well-trained audience eye is looking keenly for the story under the surface.'[31] The type of story, the kinds of characters and the style of a play set up an active relationship, a kind of agreed game which, at its most basic, means comedy will invite laughter and tragedy tears, but which also operates in more complex dimensions.

Genre

Many plays fail to fit the watertight categories plied by television and cinema with their familiar tropes – the crime and medical dramas, romcom, horror or action movies – that have become almost comforting because we know what to expect. As spectators, we seem to be programmed to anticipate outcomes, and our brains tend automatically to leap to logical conclusions. This is perhaps why the 'thriller' is such an enticing genre because we know a game is being played with our anticipatory perceptions. We want to know 'whodunnit', but confronted with a thriller, we are aware of our propensity to use logic, when what is actually required is 'thinking outside the box'.

Genre is tied to fashions of a period and develops over time, so modern farce is related to Restoration Comedy, for example. Playwrights often defy or toy with expectations of the familiar, ignoring conventions associated with well-known genres or turning them on their head. *Hamlet* is a famous example, with Shakespeare taking the popular form of his day, i.e. the potboilers called 'tragedies of blood' or Revenge Tragedies, and playing with the expectations of the audience to create something less formulaic. Since the Second World War, dramatists have increasingly pushed the boundaries of traditional forms, so that rather than fitting a specific genre, plays more often contain echoes and borrowings from a range of genres and frequently subvert traditional patterns and related meanings. Beckett is possibly the most notorious of these, labelling his play *Waiting for Godot* a tragicomedy.

'As a set of expectations of storyline, character, locale and outcome. Genre is the possession not of the writer but of the audience.'[32]

David Edgar

Familiarity with certain genres is not necessarily a turn-off. There's enjoyment from knowing how it will turn out in the end when the story is told in an engaging way. Predictability is the potential enemy. We may know it will end in tears, but we still want to relive the experience and suspense. It is the unexpected, whether in the story itself or the way it is told, that keeps us hooked. Surprise is an elementary form of pleasure, from the child's delight in turning the page of a picture book and finding something unexpected, to the plot twists of adult crime writers. Surprise is not purely reliant on the mechanics of a plot; it comes also from visual, musical, physical elements, the whole arsenal of theatricality, how a style of performance brokers a relationship between the play and the audience, enabling something memorable to be forged between them. So treating every play you work on as though it is hot off the press means surprising yourself and your potential audience even when you think you know the play and/or they know the play. Jacques Lecoq suggests, 'One should not be afraid, faced with a great theatre text, to push it around a little... without premeditation, without an opinion, as if it were being discovered for the first time.'[33]

There is nothing worse than being precious or reverential about the perceived style of a play; labels mislead if taken superficially to indicate genre or style. Huge benefits can be found in seeking lightness in the darker moments, for example, or darkness lurking beneath the apparently frivolous. John Wright suggests a rethink: 'Comedy and tragedy are unhelpful distinctions,' he writes, and 'rather than being opposite sides of a coin, they're just equal parts of the whole.'[34] Uncovering a comedic dimension in a tragedy, or tragic overtones in a play ostensibly billed as a comedy, gives complexity its head, particularly for so-called 'serious drama', where allowing contradictions to emerge adds richness. Peter Brook revealed a darker play beneath the surface comedy of *A Midsummer Night's Dream* in his 1968 production with the RSC. Arthur Miller's *A View from the Bridge* is usually billed as a 'modern tragedy', yet for him the best production was a revival directed by Alan Ayckbourn, who says he rarely laughed so much in a rehearsal room, 'as we searched both for the light, the genuinely legitimate moments of laughter – we found lots – and for speed.'[35] This production ran about thirty minutes shorter than a previous one in New York. Even in the dire circumstances created by Sarah Kane in *Blasted*, humour is never far away; as Ian prepares to shoot himself he takes the gun from his mouth and says to Cate, 'Don't stand behind me', reminding her (and the audience) that she might get splattered when he pulls the trigger. This kind of contrast energises an audience, we become more actively engaged. For empathy is 'far more robust than we think', audiences 'welcome... emotional agility', and 'we're perfectly capable of laughing and crying at the same time... once we believe that blood has been spilt, we bring the appropriate gravitas to the scene.'[36]

There are ways in which echoes and borrowings in a play can be played with and even subverted through interpretation. Shakespeare is frequently subjected to revisioning and reworking as

'Laughter is not always bad in a tragedy nor is seriousness in a comedy.'[37]

Sam Mendes

each generation reinvents his plays for new audiences, sometimes making us re-evaluate a play, sometimes not. We may sneer at the seventeenth-century rewriting of *King Lear* to give it a happy ending, but future generations may be bemused by a twenty-first century *Hamlet* set in a mental asylum, even though the contemporary audience loved it. 'Concept' productions can be thrilling if the spirit of the play is intact but also intrusive if the heart of the play is submerged. For Caryl Churchill, a playtext is 'like a blueprint which you can do different ways, so you don't go expecting it to be the same', yet when confronted with a production of *Top Girls* in Cologne where the waitress 'slunk about in a catsuit like a bunny girl', she was, understandably, moved to describe it as a 'complete travesty'.[38]

'Great plays are great plays because they survive the tampering of idiots over centuries.'[39]

Glenda Jackson

Frantic Assembly launched an electrifying adaptation of Shakespeare's *Othello* with the tagline 'a gripping thriller-tragedy'. Set in the pool room at the back of a working-class pub, their version came styled with high-voltage

physical choreography and a pulsing underscore of tracks by Hybrid. The youth of the cast ensured this was an interpretation targeted at Frantic's fan base, bringing a 'cool-ness' with popular appeal, making Shakespeare relevant in giving the play a contemporary urban setting. Earlier in its existence, the company encountered difficulties when staging a stylised version of Osborne's *Look Back in Anger*, aiming to change preconceptions of the play as naturalistic and counter what they describe as 'flat-pack theatre'. In doing so they put their company under threat since they failed to realise that legalities are attendant on adapting a play still within copyright.[40] With hindsight they recognise their adaptation 'while aiming to find the original fire at the heart of the play, was less than respectful to the existing text.'[41] Challenging or subverting expectations is best restricted to plays out of copyright.

Kaos Theatre picked a play with no such restrictions when they rendered a vibrantly stylised version of *The Importance of Being Earnest*, with high-octane physicality and clowning to underline Wilde's satirical lampooning of the upper classes. While they retained the essence of the original without adapting it, their production challenged received views about it as a formal, well-made play, presenting the play through the prism of the grotesque.

The self-styled 'immersive theatre' company Punchdrunk frequently use classical texts, and have based productions on Shakespeare's *The Tempest*, *Macbeth* and *Romeo and Juliet*. They deconstruct not only the plays themselves but what might be considered time-honoured stylistic conventions, mounting daring productions that combine performance, art installation and dance in site-specific venues. They also deconstruct the audience as everyone is issued with a half-mask to wear as they wander through the venue, opening drawers or doors to discover something that can feel as if it has been made just for them. *Sleep No More* is the title of their reworking of *Macbeth* as a Hitchcock thriller, taking over a Victorian school and inviting audiences to piece together the story in a series of individual scenes. Their first foray into production was Büchner's *Woyzeck* in 2000, and in 2013 they returned to this play, using it as the basis for *The Drowned Man: A Hollywood Fable* set over four vast floors of the old GPO building in St Pancras.

> 'Genre is breaking down, and the margins between reality and illusion are continually being eroded.'[42]
>
> John Wright

Woyzeck defies genre. Büchner's play is often referred to as 'the first modern drama', possibly because its structure – a swift-flowing sequence of scenes with a cinematic feel, telling the story of a poor soldier's descent into despair – is more akin to plays of the post-war period than the early-nineteenth century when it was written.[43] The order of scenes is provisional since Büchner died of typhus before completing it; it is claimed as naturalistic by some and expressionistic by others. As such it has inspired a host of wildly different versions in numerous theatrical modes, including a small ensemble production directed by Sarah Kane at the Gate Theatre in 1997; Thomas Ostermeier's 2004 production for the Avignon Festival, which transposed the play to an underworld on the Eastern European margins where humans are regularly trafficked; a fiendishly acrobatic version, with music by the rock musician Nick Cave, performed and directed by Gísli Örn Gardarsson in 2008; and a highly original Korean production, using a teetering pile of chairs and a score by Piazzolla, which played the London International Festival of Mime in 2010. These few examples show how incredibly malleable the play is. When the visionary director Robert Wilson created his version in 2000, he cut the text drastically and replaced much of it with music and lyrics by Tom Waits and Kathleen Brennan. The narrative backbone of the play remained while the songs – sometimes bittersweet, sometimes more vicious – transposed the central love story, allowing the tale of Woyzeck and Marie to resonate in a modern world. Waits's voice, with his signature sardonic and smoky tone, became a virtual soundtrack underscoring the hallmarks of Wilson's visually stunning theatre: vibrant colours and light, sharply defined physicality, every element of theatre integrated into a surreal whole. At repeated moments, Woyzeck ran on the spot very fast and then around the stage in a highly stylised manner, his head projecting forward and his limbs pumping like a piston engine. Such a physical demonstration of desperation and inner torment crystallised the central core of Büchner's play.[44]

Büchner was 'an extraordinary writer, with a forensic psychological insight and a tremendous feeling for romance.'[45]

Howard Brenton

It is unlikely that Büchner started out with a particular genre or style in mind, although it is clear he was inspired by the story of the real Woyzeck, a man charged with the murder of his lover in the 1820s. When this man claimed he heard voices urging him to kill, his execution was postponed for medical investigation. The story was followed avidly in the papers and when he was pronounced sane and hanged, arguments about the diagnosis went on for several years. Büchner, a student of medicine, championed the idea of telling stories of ordinary people. He was passionate about social reform, angered by the way the poor working classes were regarded merely as 'useful objects' by those in the social hierarchy, like the Captain and Doctor in the play. He joined others at his university in Giessen to form a Society for Human Rights, the first German Communist organisation. Like Brecht and Edward Bond, he recognised that, in a society based on oppression, the oppressed turn on their own, a recognition which fuelled his writing and is threaded through this play.

Theme

'"Theme" is the soil in which the narrative is rooted.'[46]

Noel Greig

Playwrights begin with an idea, maybe inspired by a person or story as Büchner was, maybe inspired by something as simple as a phrase heard or image seen, something which, as they chew it over, encapsulates things they feel they need to say or conflicting ideas they wish to expose. Whether the material lends itself to a particular genre or not, whether they end up creating a new form or reinventing an old one, whatever the end result, their play embraces that original idea. This is what is meant by the notion of a 'central core', or the answer to the question, 'What's it really about?' By the time the play is scripted, this has become embedded as the theme, working like a kind of metaphorical glue holding everything in place.

Theme is woven into the texture of a play, its visual imagery and actions as well as its language, running through it like letters through a stick of seaside rock, so that wherever you cut or stop there will be evidence of its presence. Caryl Churchill's play *Top Girls* tells the story of a mother who leaves her daughter unacknowledged because the child would restrict her ambition, a story rooted in debates about women in the workplace. The play explores dilemmas facing women balancing career aspirations and motherhood, and these topics crop up in the conversations around the table in the restaurant in Act One. Problems of equality in the workplace, the drudgery of domesticity and familial responsibility, how capitalism breeds cynicism in the wake of ambition are concerns that permeate the play. The title is not without irony; *Top Girls* is both the name of the agency where Marlene works and the embodiment of the play's central question, articulated by Churchill herself: 'What use is female emancipation… if it transforms the clever women into predators and does nothing for the stupid, weak and helpless?'[47] This question is not debated directly in dialogue but lodged in the minds of the spectators through the action as it unfolds to reveal the glamorous world of professional women is founded on betrayal, and the attitudes of the successful as questionable. This question is encapsulated in the final poignant image of the daughter Angie coming downstairs after a nightmare; her final words – 'Frightening.' 'Frightening.' – sum up the theme of the play.

'My plays have a beginning in my mind and my heart, be it six months or six years before I put it onto paper.'[48]

Sarah Kane

Whether a play is narrative-driven or not, the 'controlling' or central idea is what it is really about. In a fully fledged play this reverberates as though some invisible echo-chamber is at work behind the scenes. Unless a play is avowedly about an 'issue', such as those written by the Suffragettes to promote understanding and debate about their cause, or agitprop plays of the 1930s and 1970s, themes are more implicit than explicit. However non-explicit the themes, interpretation relates to what is going on in the world at the time. A salutary example is Arthur Miller's *A View from the Bridge*. When the play first appeared on Broadway, it was viewed as a parable about McCarthyism: Eddie's telephone call to the authorities was seen as an analogy for those accused of 'naming names', with the insinuation that Miller was castigating those who had named Communist sympathisers during the McCarthy trials.[49] When Peter Brook directed the London production of the play, it had to be shown initially under 'club conditions' since the Lord Chamberlain, then responsible for censorship, refused a performing licence because the play was widely considered to be about homosexuality, an opinion reflecting the homophobia prevalent in the 1950s.

Once the central idea takes root, the process for the writer is much the same as in devising, where companies set up improvisations with raw material before embarking on fixing the order, except that playwrights generally

'As a general principle, situation, story and character all form themselves in the writer's head before the dialogue emerges.'[50]

Noel Greig

do this on their own, unless they are working collaboratively with actors in rehearsal.[51] Either way, the dialogue is most often the last thing they write, and certainly the last to be fixed.

The physical act of writing the script can be done very quickly – John Osborne rattled off *Look Back in Anger* in just over a fortnight – but more often it is the result of a period of gestation, sometimes amounting to years. It was six or so years after hearing the story of a longshoreman who squealed to the Immigration Bureau officials about two illegal immigrants living under his roof, in order to prevent one of them marrying his niece, when Miller wrote his first version of *A View from the Bridge* as a one-act play. Once committed to an idea, Alan Ayckbourn takes a year to go through a process of working out narrative, time, location and characters before writing the actual play. Starting points vary with individual playwrights, as do methods; mature writers with several plays under their belt might work instinctively, although it is usual for several drafts to be written before finalising a script.

'Dialogue is "the sprinkles on the ice cone".'[52]

David Mamet

Many crafting manuals advise the practice of working from a synopsis to a scenario, creating an outline plan well before writing the actual dialogue, first summing up the story in prose, then laying out how it will be told scene by scene. Often playwrights are commissioned to write a play after submitting a 'treatment', where the central idea is expressed in terms of the way the narrative unfolds and how the characters illustrate the idea through what they do. Scripting the dialogue and directions become the last phase in the process, so what you read on the published page is the 'top line' of the dramatist's score.

The idea of reducing a play to a scenario and working with and from the understanding of its structural nature, rather than tackling the play head-on through negotiating the dialogue, is how this book suggests you proceed, a process which starts with mapping the play. This is akin to how directors who value actors as creative co-creators work, like Joan Littlewood: a process which puts players in the role of co-authoring, with the added bonus of sharpening an understanding of how plays are engineered and gaining insights into the skill and craft of playwriting. Getting to grips with this at the beginning of rehearsals is hugely valuable: exploring how a play works develops a deeper and fuller grasp of its underbelly and lays a foundation for more detailed investigations. Section 3: Mapping the Play contains practical work to develop this. What follows here is a preface to that work, outlining principles of structure and the importance of time in theatre for those who may be unfamiliar with them.

Structure

Apart from the intricacies of story and characters, or the events embedded in the words on the page, plays have equally significant material hidden within. And you could say that this is where the play speaks without talking, because it is the order in which each event or word occurs and their placing in relation to each other that becomes a critical element in keeping audiences enthralled. How a playwright treats the raw material, the way everything is put together, becomes this overall design or structure, invisible yet vitally important. It governs how the audience sees the play unfold in time.

A play's inherent design creates a context for narrative and emotional logic. It gives an audience threads to follow so that they are neither baffled nor distracted. Yet it is invisible once the play is performed. A medieval tapestry or Persian rug is a pertinent analogy since the original threads on the loom are not seen once the coloured wools have worked their magic. Playwrights rely on directing the audience's attention through the actions, visual images and words that become embodied in performance, and – just as importantly – their placing. The way these elements are set up, combined and balanced in relation to audience expectations is how we begin asking certain questions and, eventually, move towards possible answers. And the way these elements are organised provides the structure.

'A script articulates and orchestrates incidents, ideas and feelings into a satisfying and meaningful structure.'[53]

John Wright

'A piece of writing is a structure in motion.'[54]

Jacques Lecoq

Structure is as deliberate a way of conveying meaning and emotion as plot or theme or character, as central to its impact as what the play is about, who features in it and how it works visually. View it as the bones of a play, the skeleton on which muscles, nerves, limbs and features depend, but a skeleton energised in the sense that it dictates when and how the body of the play springs to life and the directions in which it moves. Despite being invisible it affects the way audiences respond and engage with the play, like a secret life planted in the text which comes out of hiding when the play is performed. When a play works through a problem, moving from question to answer, problem to potential solution with the audience's involvement increasing as more questions are raised, the way its structure is embedded provokes those questions. When classic narrative structures are deployed, the questions tend to revolve around the 'what will happen next?' Alternative structures, as apparent in *Waiting for Godot* and *Blasted*, for example, can steer us towards asking 'what does this mean?'

'The deeper the questions, the more complex and satisfying the story will be for the audience.'[55]

Noel Greig

Addressing the question 'what is a good drama?', the American playwright and director David Mamet uses the analogy of a dirty joke: 'The dirty-joke teller is tending toward a punchline and we know that he or she is only going to tell us the elements which direct our attention toward that punchline, so we listen attentively'.[56] The example of a visual gag or a conjurer's trick offers a similar analogy, one that focuses on what we see. A play in performance unfolds for us gradually: it is not simply what we see happening or hear said that affects us but the fact that everything moves forward in time. We watch attentively, aware of when anything on stage changes – when it does, whether incrementally or very suddenly, we sit up and take notice.

> '*Structure is not just a convenient way of organising material, but is a conveyer of meaning.*'[57]
>
> David Edgar

Structure becomes the way a dramatist positions the audience in relation to what the play is about. In a linear, narrative-based plot, it is fairly straightforward to trace the changes that occur during the course of the play and the various states of turmoil these provoke as events unfold. Each change upsets the previous balance and creates a new one; the new one is not necessarily better, nevertheless characters have to adjust to it. The arrangement of events and their consequences in a conventional form tends to lead the audience to a preferred conclusion, with the audience persuaded to see the outcome as inevitable. In plays with little obvious narrative, theme may take precedence yet there is a continuous sense of movement: the principle of events disturbing or shifting the balance and different ones emerging still applies, although outcomes are less obvious and can embrace levels of ambiguity which question any comfortable conclusion.

Suspense

The structure of a play is designed to reveal characters: their individual actions and reactions are deliberate dramatic choices organised and orchestrated to serve the narrative and/or theme, and channelled through the plotting, plan or design for the way in which the play will unfold. Dramatic action can be a confusing concept; it is really about creating suspense, building and slackening tension in order to keep the audience involved, and this is where the internal dynamics of a play reside. It is often compared to compositional structure in music, since music also moves forward in time. In jazz and classical music, effects are achieved through manipulating tensions in the rhythm and melodic lines to maintain the listener's attention. With electronic music, it is how the number of beats per minute increases and decreases – what's called the BPM, and it is this that causes heart rates to speed up or slow down in response.

A conventional structure means the dramatic action is designed to sweep us up on a tide which seems to have its own internal rhythm of rising and falling – moments of anticipation and expectation, moments of surprise and deflation. As it progresses, we become more and more engrossed in what's happening on stage, until finally, almost as though a puzzle has been solved, the ending arrives. The undercurrents eddying beneath the main storyline turn watching into a dynamic process, with smaller struggles and conflicts contributing to the whole.

Seeing a play where our attention is engaged in this way means curiosity is not only aroused but gradually deepens. The aim is to grab the audience's attention and not only hang on to it but intensify their involvement, and it is in the states of tension where the success or failure resides, the push and pull of suspense and release creating balance and counterbalance. Recognising this becomes particularly relevant in the latter stages of a rehearsal process when attending to the rhythmic patterning of performance, and this is dealt with in the final section of this book, Section 8: Shaping and Pacing.

> *'The play is a quest for a solution.'*[58]
>
> David Mamet

A constant on-the-edge-of-seat suspense can be very wearing and not necessarily desirable, yet audiences are eager to discover what's happening, why it's happening, what will happen next, what has happened, and what it all means. The dramatist ekes out the answers, planting clues for us to decipher, sometimes giving half-answers to add intrigue or set up further questions, sometimes using only a single line, action or visual image to alert us to a change in circumstance. Terms used by writers are 'plants and pay-offs' or 'fuses and bombs', actions and events placed to detonate in the narrative, or signal thematic concerns; the screenwriter Michael Eaton calls this process 'choreographing knowledge',[59] a phrase we will return to, as it captures the placing and timing of incidents, images and utterances in the preparation of a play for performance.

When he defined the elements of drama in his *Poetics*, Aristotle placed them in an order with Plot preceding Character and followed by Language, Thought, Spectacle and Music. His emphasis on plot is considered conservative when referred to as the way in which narrative incidents are ordered. But this is a rather simplistic interpretation. Theatre director Peter Hall points out that the word plot in Greek is 'the vexed word "Muthos": vexed because it is one of those portmanteau Greek words which means a multitude of things – story, narrative, myth, theme...'[60] In this sense, plot is more akin to the definition of structure and the idea of a plot as a 'secret plan'. The issue of conservatism lies more in the fact that Aristotle's formula for constructing plots insists on organising material in chronological order with events moving forward in linear progression; the story appears to be 'going somewhere' since it is reinforced by a time-structure which is also moving forwards. His maxim of 'unity of time and place' arose from his study of Greek plays of the fifth century, as is evident, for instance, in *Antigone*, where everything happens in a short time span outside the palace. These plays condensed time to intensify the dramatic action, often into a single day. Dramatists since the Greeks have treated time as more elastic: time can be contracted, or stopped; it can jump – forwards or backwards – and even seem stretched. So time-structure does not simply mean the external clock or calendar time of events; it is a kind of 'internal-yet-total-time' specific to the play, where time on the inside does not necessarily operate like real time.

Time

The way time is structured is a key factor in the audience experience. Plays that compress time, placing events and their

'[A play is] a space of time that is always filled with moving.'[61]

Gertrude Stein

consequences to serve dramatic effect, tend to intensify audience involvement. A common strategy employed in playwriting to produce a sense of urgency in the action is to 'put a clock on a scene', for example, imposing some kind of deadline for a character to make a decision. Shorter time spans press home the need for a solution or resolution of some kind. Longer time spans seem to bring about a distancing effect, placing events in perspective through the lens of an extended period. It could be argued that this is inherent in Brecht's theory of epic theatre. *Mother Courage and Her Children* covers many years of the Thirty Years War, dropping in on key moments in Mother Courage's journey. It is 1624 when she sets out to drag her cart behind the army; by 1636, she has crossed many territorial borders, changing sides when necessary to survive financially, and paid the price in losing her children.

Time, character and plot are the traditional crutches of narrative drama. What happens when those are kicked away? Various experiments in theatre have offered a powerful reaction against what is perceived in postmodern criticism as the tyranny of classical linear narrative. In his experiment on *Hamlet* in 1965 with Charles Marowitz, Peter Brook dismantled the play and reconstructed it as direct expression without the linearity of narrative, and, in so doing, came to the conclusion that, despite all the other structural possibilities that exist, 'narrative is the most powerful of them all'.[62] In identifying suspense as the key to the power in drama, he observed this is not the suspense inherent in 'what happens next?' but in how time operates, the way in which linear time can be criss-crossed with 'internal time', 'dream time', 'psychological time', like currents eddying around the strength of the narrative, and which can be embodied and realised theatrically.

While pre-twentieth-century playwrights tended to follow linear and chronological paths with an overarching narrative, albeit with plenty of variety in the patterning and shaping of a play's internal structures, playwrights in the twentieth century inched increasingly towards abstraction, much as did painters, sculptors and novelists. We are now familiar with dramatic structures that avoid straightforward linear progression, plays which are less dependent on narrative as the primary driver. The obvious example is *Waiting for Godot*; its first performances were met with bewilderment, and the phrase 'nothing happens – twice' from an early review of the play is much quoted. But the structure of Beckett's play is more akin to music, its composition closer to a fugue where theme and variations play out through counterpoint. In *Waiting for Godot*, stage time runs almost in parallel to auditorium time, since the spectators are caught up in a sense of waiting along with the performers on stage. It is only when the audience starts realising the second act has an almost identical structure to the first that meaning begins to emerge, and this realisation tallies with the situation of the characters, constantly reliving the hope and despair of waiting for the elusive Godot.

Time is measured in Bond's *Saved*, engineered so an audience has to work out what has happened in the gaps between scenes – a skilful way of keeping them very focused as they piece together events that have occurred in the interim. It is nonetheless dramatic for all the apparent slowness of the unfolding narrative.

'An understanding of the drama's form always helps release the writer's intentions.'[63]

Peter Hall

Caryl Churchill and Sarah Kane are two playwrights who relish the theatrical possibilities of disrupting time. In Churchill's *Cloud Nine*, one hundred years passes between Acts One and Two but only twenty-five years in the lives of the characters; *Top Girls* opens with Marlene celebrating her managerial appointment with a variety of women from different periods of history – clearly a surreal blending of time – and Acts Two and Three reverse chronological time, with the linear story switched around so that events in Act Two occur chronologically after those in Act Three. While the time-structure is disrupted, the way the play unfolds moves the audience forward in thinking about the central question. Dramatic tension is still at work but focused less on the cause-and-effect model of unfolding events and more towards thematic concerns. Kane uses a brutal disjunction of time in *Blasted*, propelling the action from the hotel room to a war zone; the use of the sound of differing seasonal rain in between scenes adds to the sense of moving through time during the course of the play.

While the time span is disjointed in these plays, the journey of the characters still moves forward for the audience. The plots are reliant on the audience piecing together the puzzle, so the engagement of the audience is at a different and deeper level than simply following a linear narrative thread.

Style

If a play is a set of problems or a puzzle then rehearsals explore the problems and propose solutions, putting the play under practical scrutiny, and testing out possible answers. The manner in which this is approached will dictate the eventual style in which a play is presented in performance. Assumptions about a play's style are as problematic and misleading as those about genre. The idea of working through a series of exercises and gradually moving closer to the theatrical context without swamping the play, allowing ideas to develop incrementally, should, ideally, mean that style eventually finds itself, reminding us of 'Copeau's praiseworthy ideal of finding the right style for a given play and finding it only in rehearsal.'[64]

There is a metaphorical dimension to the inherent physicality of the text, an image structure working on subliminal planes both at the level of detail and within the play as a whole. This is embedded in the patterns of actions, gestures and movements, which become apparent and visible through working on these elements. Accessing and choreographing visual imagery as rehearsals progress is as significant and constantly active as choreographing the narrative. There is an ongoing journey into discovering how the play speaks on multiple levels and through layers of meaning, and this is part and parcel of discovering the style.

'The work of rehearsal should be the quest for style.'[65]

Simon Callow

The precision of players' sensuality and physicality becomes as significant as any textual or scenographic detail. And heightened physicality promotes a heightened kinaesthetic experience for the spectator: 'the tensions and modifications in the actor's body provoke an immediate effect on the body of the spectator.'[66] What Eugenio Barba refers to as a 'kinaesthetic empathy' between performers and spectators is a vital area to exploit in approaching a play. If the visible and kinaesthetic are inseparable for the spectator, the psychic and somatic are inseparable for the players. The route towards this lies in working through play.

Section 2

Serious Play

Serious Play

Theatre thrives on play. An ability to play is central to all aspects of theatre-making; the actor Simon Callow maintains that 'play is behind all great acting and all great theatre'.[67]

'Everything that occurs on the stage is linked to the idea of play and the word "play".'[68]

Simon McBurney

It is Copeau, a director of scripted plays, who first identified and explored the parallels between acting and play, inspired by watching his own children at play and recognising the powerful freedom of their imaginations. Play became a fundamental feature of his actor-training, a process of integrating the body and imagination. His research into *commedia dell'arte* led to practical explorations with mask work, and this, together with his examination of the affinity between clowning and acting, has had lasting impact. It is largely Copeau's legacy which has inspired and continues to fuel play as fundamental to theatre-making, most recently through Lecoq and 'the skills of play [that] have been articulated by the pioneering teaching of Monika Pagneux and Philippe Gaulier'.[69] For Lecoq, creativity is driven by play, with play as not only a synonym for acting/performing but also a quality his student actors are encouraged to seek out and express in their actions, reactions and interactions.

Play is also a touchstone for directors not automatically regarded as belonging in Copeau's genealogy. Contemporary theatre directors as varied as Peter Hall, Alan Ayckbourn and Emma Rice espouse the necessity of play in the rehearsal room. Brecht is seldom thought of as a director associated with play, yet George Devine commented how the actors were like children playing when he watched the Berliner Ensemble in rehearsals, and a recent book about Brecht by the director Manfred Wekwerth (who worked alongside Brecht on *Mother Courage*) is titled *Daring to Play*. Beckett is another iconic figure whose punctiliousness in directing actors to observe precisely what he wrote means he is rarely considered playful, although the advice he gave most frequently in rehearsals for *Waiting for Godot* when directing the play in Berlin was '*rein Spiel*' which means 'just play'.[70]

For Joan Littlewood, play and games were a fertile breeding ground in developing intuition, curiosity and imagination in her Theatre Workshop actors.

> '*Acting is about sharing, learning to play together.*'[71]
>
> Alan Ayckbourn

She frequently used games to generate the *mise-en-scène*, and had an unnerving instinct for employing a range of physical games and exercises to open up a text, whether a classic or newly penned, leading her actors directly to improvisations which took them right inside the play. During an extended game of Cowboys and Indians she fed in situations for them to improvise so as to bring them gradually into acquaintance with Shakespeare's *Macbeth*. One of her best-known strategies was finding parallel situations for those in a play, as when actors played The Raft of the Medusa as a springboard into creating a revolutionary Parisian mob for Büchner's *Danton's Death*, and spent hours on the roof of the Theatre Royal in Stratford East pretending to be prisoners in a prison yard for Brendan Behan's *The Hostage*, an exercise which then developed into improvisations to find the detail of cell life. What is always remarked upon by commentators about Theatre Workshop productions was how *real* the performances were, and this was a reality forged in imaginative play.

Two principles underpin Peter Brook's work: a finely tuned body and the necessity of playful improvisation. The bodies of the actors rehearsing for his famed production of *A Midsummer Night's Dream* were tuned through gymnastics and circus skills. After mornings filled with plate-spinning and stilt-walking, they did 'comic improvisations to encourage inventiveness and to taste playing for the sake of playing'; it was only towards the end of the day they fell onto cushions and read the text.[72] Play had enabled them to become highly inventive during the rehearsal process, so that when the production was up and running at Stratford, Brook took them off to London's Roundhouse to a different environment without the white-box set. The ropes and trapezes were left behind as they performed in completely new conditions, with seven hundred spectators scattered around on the concrete floors. Shakespeare's play became second nature to actors who had developed such an inbuilt rapport they could invent new moves or new acrobatic stunts on the spur of the moment, using the staircases, pillars and galleries of the building, while still telling the same story in the same words. They had learnt how to perform the play as a game, a game they could play with each other in any surroundings.

'Theatre becomes a deadly industry if a performer is not there to play.'[73]

Peter Brook

Play is not anarchic; it has rules. When everyone knows the game, there is an unwritten agreement to observe rules and comply with the restraints they impose. We play seriously even though we are having fun. A game of tag is a metaphor for the ethos of rehearsals: the desire to stay in the game requires purpose and commitment; it activates awareness of the self in space and in relation to others, sharpens reactions and the ability to respond spontaneously in the moment. Everyone is constantly on the alert, calculating their distance from the tagger and their relationship to the space and others. In the version called Stick-in-the-Mud – sometimes also called British Bulldog – another layer is introduced as tagged players are obliged to stand with their legs astride until a free player releases them by crawling through their legs. Awareness extends to noting when others become stuck and assessing the distance between yourself, them and the tagger to ensure you can free them while steering clear of being tagged yourself. Releasing others by crawling through their legs is not a generous act, simply how the game works. Players become dependent on each other, and a team spirit in the sense of 'us' against 'them' is induced; you have to be reciprocal as well as competitive with generosity operating as an additional 'rule'. If you are not released and end up taking over as the tagger, you respond according to the rules and switch to preventing anyone being released by tagging those trying to help them. Competitiveness and a certain degree of aggression are necessary and positive adjuncts in some games. Games can provide analogies for behaviour relating to characters. In this one there are opportunities to role-play being victims and allies as well as an oppressor.

'The only way you can attain creative ideas is if you play.'[74]

Robert Lepage

Play is fundamental to acting, increasing awareness of others in space and ways of communicating without verbalising; it hones the senses, and players find their physical potential and activate their spatial awareness. The actions used in play are fluid and scattered, requiring rapid responses to unplanned outcomes. Cultivating an ability to play with others builds skill and trust via shared physical and creative vocabularies where the surprising and the absurd are celebrated. In liberating players' imaginations, fostering initiative, intuition and intelligence, play develops the necessary rapport to working on stage instinctively.

A natural connection between games and acting exists: like mini-dramas, games have beginnings, middles and ends, and often embody conflict. We play them in the present tense,

'Playing encourages the release of instinctive responses.'[75]

John Harrop

and the experience is never quite the same. Simon McBurney points out that while games activate imagination, rules provide a framework where spontaneity can thrive. Sometimes the rigidity of the rule, as in the game Simple Simon Says, makes it a good exercise for concentration. In Grandmother's Footsteps, players have to test the rule of not being seen when Grandmother turns round, within the framework of the situation of not getting caught. Failure is part of the fun. There is laughter when we get it wrong. Games happen in the present moment: truly involved and engaged, you live through the experience, and no matter how often you play a game it is different every time.[76]

Play provides the conditions necessary for theatrical invention; it is as essential and as productive for text work as it is in a devising process because it opens up a space where ideas emerge not from a prescriptive plan but through spontaneous impulses. However, for play to be valuable it needs to be structured, its outcomes recognised and exploited. While games put players into a state of readiness for improvisation, beware of seeing them simply as ice-breakers or warm-ups before the main business of tackling a text. They are indispensable tools for analysis, catalysts for creativity, and they cultivate an improvisational attitude, all of which are vital elements in investigating a play. Games serve every aspect of working on a text, from exploring metaphors and analogous situations, to accessing dynamic interaction, generating action, creating imagery, working with props, and from examining subtext to discovering what drives characters and what facets or characteristics or contradictions they display. As the director John Wright states, 'Games *are* the work'.[77]

Play as work

Using a game that acts as a metaphor for the play, or a scene in a play, establishes a visceral connection with its underlying

'The subtle blending of "play" and "work" liberates the performer.'[78]

Scott Graham and Steven Hoggett

themes. Competitive games are ideal for plays where conflict is overt. A Tug of War with Creon leading one end of the rope and Antigone the other illustrates the core of that play very simply, for example, and the push-and-pull dynamic of that game can be harnessed as the dramatic motor for many of the individual scenes. The notion of push/pull as a fundamental principle of dynamics on stage is a bedrock of Lecoq's pedagogy, examined in more detail later in this section and applied in various ways through the following sections.

The choice of game is important. Those that energise players and space are most beneficial. A game like Wink Murder may be fun but provokes no urgency to move and is far too superficial for a play like *Macbeth*. A game like Marco Polo, a version of Blind Man's Bluff, works brilliantly for the forest scenes in *A Midsummer Night's Dream*. One player is blindfolded while others run around and dart towards her, whispering 'Marco Polo' as a dare for her to turn and touch them. Once 'tagged', that person becomes the new blindfolded player. Played in variations with up to four players blindfolded at any one time with the rest of the group taunting them not only creates a simple analogy for the lovers being lost in the forest, it also immediately opens up movement in the space. The level of energy required is quick and light, with the daring players getting as close to the blindfolded ones as possible without being tagged; this develops an organic sense of dynamic movement which can be translated into development work on the scenes.

Games are active. The visceral experience of playing animates players, and the right game animates the text. At a simple level, the game Sock in the Tail, where pairs try to steal their opponent's 'tail' – a sock tucked into the waistband in the middle of the back – serves to demonstrate the urgency of someone wanting something from another person, and how actively we defend ourselves. Laying dialogue from a scene where one character tries to get something from another on top of this game, with players improvising if they haven't yet learnt the dialogue, offers a 'lived in' experience to draw on for the scene, and has the potential by-product of sketching the framework of a physical score that will be far more alive than attempting to 'block' it. The physicality of playing a game releases emotional aspects of the action.

'A chorus is a body which moves organically like a living creature.' [79]

Jacques Lecoq

It is often remarked that acting is reacting. In many games we are automatically in reactive mode, responding to others in the moment. Reaction is the major element of a chorus and searching for the right emotional level to unite the crowd at key points can be a tall order. An effective chorus works like a living organism. They are not simply a crowd; there is a collective nature to a chorus, whether in a Greek play like *Antigone* or a modern one such as *A View from the Bridge* or Berkoff's *Greek*, where a sense of individuals within a group has to be coupled with unity. One game that develops this organically is Jellyfish, where a group huddle in one big heap and practise contracting and releasing their breath to achieve a sense of unison until they gradually morph into a heaving mass, applying the necessary physical discipline to be able to slither across the floor as one enormous giant jellyfish. As with all improvisatory games, it's important not to expect immediate results;

games like this repay being played many times before you reap the benefit. Commentators frequently mention the fluently choreographed moment in Complicite's *Street of Crocodiles* where actors appeared like a flock of starlings, dipping and wheeling in a mesmerising and constantly shifting formation across the stage as they flapped pages of books held at arm's length. The enormous physical discipline they executed came not only from innumerable improvisations but from how rehearsals began every day with actors playing Shoal of Fish, a game where a group literally plays at being a shoal of fish, moving as one body around the space, with leadership changing as individuals dart hither and thither and others suddenly switch direction to follow them.

Using games to unlock the action within a scene or moments in a scene is not dependent on importing known games. Finding a game between players is just what it says: finding a game between you where the reactions have a context which means they can operate at the level of meaning for an audience. One of the most valuable exercises for players is to give them a few easily available objects, e.g. plastic buckets, empty water bottles and scarves, and invite them to invent their own games. This engenders a freedom in an ensemble to apply the concept of 'finding the game' without feeling they have to import a known game, as well as bonding them through the shared enterprise of creating their own games.

Finding the game

'The discipline is to find the game that makes the reaction real – that's all.'[80]

John Wright

The concept of 'finding the game' becomes a familiar strategy in a rehearsal room when the search is for authenticity through playful improvisation. Improvisations where actors mimic human behaviour lean towards the pictorial and illustrative, with a focus on seeing things in everyday terms; this tends to limit the potential to communicate expressively as everything becomes an imitation of reality, which may well be recognisable but doesn't necessarily capture a sense of being *real*. Finding the game between players is a serious application of playfulness to gain expressiveness, making reactions real without resorting to surface imitation. The physical choices made in such games communicate intention and the physicality involved releases the emotional content of the action. Sometimes the game is overt and sometimes it operates at a more subtle level.

The cast of Kaos's production of *The Importance of Being Earnest* found the physicality of several scenes through this approach. When Cecily and Gwendolen realise they have been duped by both Jack and Algernon pretending to be called Ernest, and Jack realises that Algernon appears to be engaged to his young ward Cecily but that his own engagement to Gwendolen is in peril, the two men are left on stage to confront each other. Wilde's stage directions refer to Algernon eating muffins. The Kaos actors playing Algernon and Jack found a game in rehearsals with the tea trolley: Jack moved it around, sometimes at hair-raising speed, sometimes nonchalantly, just as Algernon reached for a muffin. A game which began as horseplay was honed during rehearsals to allow the dialogue to ride on top of the movement, and the scene was duly christened 'the muffins scene'.

Finding the game serves equally well for more disturbing scenes. Working on Scene Six of Bond's *Saved*, in which a group of lads stone a baby, student actors of mine used a standard office chair with castors for the pram and beanbags for stones. The game of pushing the pram became highly energised as they careered around the stage area, finding a push-and-pull dynamic between players and the pram. When they got to the point of stone-throwing they struggled with the idea that the pram housed a baby and their energy dissipated. Once they found a game of trying to hit the target as accurately as possible, they became remarkably competitive and discovered clear lines of physical action they were able to adopt and adapt to marry those demanded by the writing. Through finding that game they felt empowered to play the situation to maximum dramatic effect without concerning themselves with the appalling nature of it. Freed from thinking about the disturbing nature of the scene, their actions and reactions took on a lifelike reality. They had tapped into a dynamic energy at the core of that scene that seemed

> 'The rules of the game in poetic creation are in the playing itself.'[81]
>
> Jacques Lecoq

all the more horrific when they realised afterwards how much they had enjoyed themselves.

Finding the game can also bring life to the detail of small moments. 'Games amplify action' is John Wright's motto,[82] pointing out that actors accustomed to planning objectives can often find they end up with a lack of convincing interaction. Planning objectives is cerebral, a game makes them active. He cites an example of two student actors working on a scene between an extremely controlling and potentially violent husband and his timid wife in Jim Cartwright's *Two*. They had successfully worked out the action and atmosphere but needed more interaction between the couple. Wright asked them to find the game of the husband 'allowing her to come to her seat' after she'd visited the toilets. They played the same actions they had already developed but, as the actor playing the husband stared into his pint, he began holding his breath and only when he breathed out was the wife allowed to return to her seat. Holding his breath was an actual restriction which made him look as though he was trying to control his temper. She was forced to actually wait which meant she was in reality letting him control her. In the simple game of breathing and waiting they found a new dynamic and edge, making the scene more active and more alive.[83]

What becomes clear in both these illustrations is how it is the *situation* that is being played, rather than any complex psychological process or emotional state.

Hiding the game

'The plot gives you the dramatic context but the game gives us the life of the interaction.'[84]

John Wright

The delight of inventing new games or playing familiar ones arrives from the sensation of being 'in the moment'. There's immediacy and spontaneity which is part of the pleasure of play, a pleasure which can be infectious when audiences recognise a game is being played. The tea-trolley game in Kaos's *Earnest* is recognisably a game to be enjoyed at the level of a comic routine, and the game is more or less declared where part of the pleasure for the audience comes from watching the physical dexterity of the actors. The game of breathing Wright describes and the game of accurate stone-throwing in *Saved* are not overt; in these instances the games the actors play are hidden from the audience, essentially creating dramatic illusion. While finding the game in rehearsal serves to invigorate objectives for the actors, the audience read it in performance on a more psychological level as a convincing portrayal of particular characters in a particular situation. Advising players to 'be more boring' when their acting teeters over into the melodramatic is a useful application of the principle of 'hiding the game', not least because it alerts them to the fact that playing feelings is also a game.

Play and the body

As human beings we read bodies. Maybe we do that before we learn to talk. We understand a person's feelings in the way their body expresses something,

'The capacity for instant, powerful, controlled reaction is a recognisable attribute of acting.'[85]

John Harrop

how it conveys an internal sensation. Our observance of physicalisation enables us to discern emotion and detect what a character is thinking. David Lan, Artistic Director of the Young Vic, says he 'discovered, and can't really say why this should be, that movement of the body – either the whole or part of the body – in the right way and at the right time in a controlled way, appears to convey to an audience what is happening in the mind of the actor.'[86]

We read a complex set of ideas in a character, not merely what they are feeling at a particular point in the play. The body conveys thoughts and ideas and feelings and reactions at one and the same time. A performer uses their entire body. Acting doesn't only happen from the chest up; everything from what your toes or fingers get up to, or how you place your foot, transmits signals and tells stories. Wherever the body is, how tense or relaxed the body is, whatever the body is doing from the slightest gesture to the fear or rage or joy of a crowd, it is movement that conveys meaning in the context of its place in the structure of the story. Spectators will invest any movement, or lack of it, with meaning. From the tiniest gesture to the biggest leap, movement on stage cannot be arbitrary, it needs control to have a desired effect.

'For a body to be able to listen motionless, it must first be developed in movement.'[87]

Peter Brook

Theatre with the idea of dance at its centre does not necessarily mean actually dancing but it does rely on alert and flexible bodies that can engage actively in play.

The spine is a major channel for distributing impulses, the pelvis works like spaghetti junction as a centre where nerve endings meet breath control via the diaphragm, and these areas need to be mobile to allow deft, unhindered movement of joints and limbs and head. Playing through the body wakes us up, opens up possibilities, often inspiring us to take creative risks and, ultimately, to have the confidence to transform in a manner that resonates physically. Ignore the body and, as Peter Brook points out, 'one is doomed to draw ideas from the overfamiliar and well-used regions of the brain at the expense of more creative levels'.[88]

There is a kind of empowerment in working through the body and engaging with other bodies, and a sense of experimenting with 'what can I do?' and 'what can we do together?' when work is playful. Sometimes this can change an actor's perceptions about their body and their ability to achieve. Commitment to working through the body brings a focus on energy as a vital ingredient and develops the skills to inhabit an emotional space physically. The physical isn't necessarily more truthful than the spoken word but has an edginess, a sense of danger and risk that attracts attention. The actors in Eugenio Barba's Odin theatre company make a personal investment in training prompted by curiosity, working through exercises designed to eliminate resistances, allowing points of difficulty to become a focus for investigation rather than stumbling blocks to be overcome. Rigorous training such as Frantic Assembly use is nonetheless personal, aiming not for technical perfection but to explore ways in which performers can find emotional truth through physical deftness. Kneehigh and Complicite play various ball games in their breaks; in addition to the physical benefits for bodies, reactions and teamwork, these give players time to recharge their creative batteries and digest the ideas developed during rehearsals.

Rather than what he calls 'comforting' gymnastic methods – comforting because they make participants feel better – students of Lecoq's school are versed in connecting observation and imagination in preparing their bodies. To avoid falling into the trap of only acquiring technique, the analysis of movement and gesture is slotted into playful dramatised sequences: a somersault becomes an expression of elation on winning a prize, for example, or the sequence of movements and attitudes involved in miming climbing over a gate becomes part of a scenario of being chased while escaping from a crime. In what he called 'animal gymnastics', Lecoq made use of animal analogies to loosen specific muscles: cat movements for flexible spines, lions and tigers for shoulder blades and 'elongation of the spine with reference to meerkats standing guard in the desert'.[89] A visit to the zoo to conduct detailed investigations of how animals connect with the ground, close examination of the animals' attitudes and pace of movement would be followed not merely by applying observational skills to render animal characteristics through the body, but imagining the floor burning hot so whether playing a flat-footed bear or a web-footed duck actors could 'discover the dynamics of that particular walk'.[90]

Spontaneity and playfulness lie at the heart of Lecoq's creative pedagogy where the relationship between movement and imagination is never forgotten: 'My method aims to promote the emergence of a theatre where the actor is playful. It is a theatre of movement, but above all a theatre of imagination.'[92] In educating actors through their bodies, he applied a forensic analysis of movement and employed principles of mime to 'teach actors who also used words to rely more heavily on the visual, expressive use of gesture, and to help them realise that often what the body was doing could say as much or more than any words.'[93]

> 'There is no such thing as an intelligent head. There is a whole composite which knows and mimes through its whole body.'[91]
>
> Jacques Lecoq

Mime and gesture

For Lecoq, playfulness was underpinned by a serious approach to searching for a language of gesture not tied to surface imitation. It is important to understand his concept of mime and gesture in this context. It does not mean those indicative gestures we use to replace language when words cannot be heard or understood, as when we try to communicate over the noise of traffic or in a foreign country; such grimaces and gesticulations are tied to literal thinking, explanatory rather than expressive, mimicry rather than mime. At the heart of Lecoq's search lies the potential to find gestures that are not simply copies of behaviour but sourced in an imaginative realm.

'The theatre of gesture and image welcomes the different possibilities that mime offers.'[94]

Jacques Lecoq

He rejects the notion of mime as imitation or representation. His concept of mime is to grasp the real through embodiment. Observation as a key dimension spreads from animals to things, exploring elements like lead and water, fire and granite, natural substances like oil and custard. The Lecoq student undertakes physical improvisations of active materials, such as a sugar cube dissolving or a plastic bag blown by the wind, in their quest to discover the inner dynamics of the natural world. In the crumpling of paper or the melting of sugar there is an essential passivity, for example. This kind of observation is one that goes beneath the surface and beyond the everyday. The idea of laying down circuits in the body in this manner is central to Lecoq's training, with traces of what he calls this 'identification work' remaining 'forever engraved in the body of the actor', so that when s/he later encounters a text 'the text will set up resonances in the body, meeting rich deposits awaiting expressive formulation so the actor can then speak from full physical awareness'.[95] It might mean approaching the movement of the Ghost in *Hamlet* through the sensation of moving like lava, for example.

It is in the primary core of what Lecoq calls 'push-and-pull' that the search for internal dynamics resides. As a sports coach and physical-education specialist

'To mime is to literally embody and therefore to understand better.'[96]

Jacques Lecoq

prior to discovering theatre, Lecoq was heavily influenced by Georges Hébert, whose methodology is recognised as the source/inspiration for outdoor-pursuit training and the idea of the modern obstacle course. Hébert's 'natural gymnastics' had influenced Copeau's physical training for actors, while Lecoq took this further to focus on the primary core element of Hébert's ten activities: 'push-and-pull'. He identifies the manifestation of mime through the body in three phases: 'agent', 'acting', and 'acted on'. And this is predicated on the basis of three modes of physical action:

'I push or I pull

I push or pull myself

I am pushed or I am pulled.'[97]

Anyone familiar with contact improvisation will understand this in terms of the necessary give-and-take that operates between partners in order to move. If one pushes the other has to give, if both partners push nobody goes anywhere. The idea of opening-up space between players as metaphorical elastic is based on this principle. When translated to the individual, the push-and-pull dynamic operates within the body, and the exercise *Animal on a lead* in Section 4 explores this in relation to pulling or being pulled by an imaginary animal. The following exercise explores this interior push/pull dynamic in a playful game.

Playing drunk

Line up five or six players facing away/upstage with their backs to the audience.

Each individual player in the line walks towards the back of the stage to epitomise coming home after a night on the tiles; when they arrive near the rear wall/curtain they attempt to find the door key on their person and open the door.

This is a non-verbal exercise although grunts and sighs are permitted.

Once the initial hilarity dies down, invite the audience to state the degree to which any player convinced them of the situation. Then replay until all the players have had a go.

Each time you discuss what 'works' and what doesn't, consider the way players use their bodies. The trick is to realise that the drunk wants to go forward – that's their motivation, if you like – while their inebriated body struggles to go in that direction, and pulls them back or sideways. Similarly with the key – the drunk wants to put the key in the lock but their hand seems to have a will of its own and is pulled every which way.

'When you walk downstage you do not think about walking downstage; you think about not walking upstage.'[98]

Anne Bogart

The notion of a push/pull dynamic is fundamental. Here again the word 'play' has additional connotations – we talk of the 'play' in a piece of elastic to express the way it expands and contracts. This push/pull dynamic is fundamental to kinaesthetic understanding of how characters can feel pushed or pulled in opposing directions, whether by external things beyond their control or subconscious desires. It lies at the core of acting a play.

'Games, actions and rehearsal exercises are like ladders which help you reach your performance and eventually get kicked away,' writes Harriet Walter, and points out an added bonus in drawing together individual players, 'into a mutually committed team.'[99] Playing them, enjoying them, using them, valuing them is essential to serious work on a scripted play. They tap into what McBurney describes as the 'artery of the imagination', opening up choices and possibilities that serve deeper connections between a company or group and the play itself.

Section 3

Mapping a Play

Mapping a Play

Mapping is the first stage in building a relationship with a scripted play as active partners. It puts the concept of a play-as-landscape into action, giving a 'global view' of the whole before exploring how individual parts fit together.

'We do not read the play. We tell the story, breaking it into themes and structures.'[100]

Emma Rice

As discussed in Section 1, it is structural elements that govern the continuity of a play and its inherent cumulative nature. Mapping is a way of making sense of a play's progression, encouraging a connection with its 'secret life' by unearthing those elements in order to garner a shared knowledge of a play's overall patterning and shape, its interior dynamics. The progression of incidents, whether chronological or not, is one dimension to uncover, yet there is also a lateral dimension encompassing tangential meanings as the play spreads out. The forward drive to a narrative works like gearing to propel a story forward, while its differential drive modifies speed and direction to encompass thematic and metaphorical aspects. Using image-making and storytelling techniques to fuel discoveries lays foundations for a deeper engagement with the play, giving access to both these dimensions. Understanding comes via embodied and shared experience within an ensemble as players gain an overall perspective on the whole play; this makes rehearsals far more productive later when getting to grips with the text in detail. At the start of rehearsals, Annabel Arden gets actors to stand up and tell the story of the play in five to fifteen minutes 'because if you don't understand what you're performing in its overall sweep, you can never really articulate its meaning as a member of an ensemble.'[101]

Instead of starting with a readthrough and working through it scene by scene from the beginning, treat the play in a similar way to raw material for devising, working actively with initial impressions, especially those features which strike play-

'I don't worry about detail so much early on, I'm more interested in exploring all sorts of different alleyways within the process.'[102]

Sam Mendes

ers as surprising or significant at first reading. Sketching out imagery and action allows the play to live more readily in shared visual and physical encounters before attempting work on dialogue.

Working with space

Since players occupy and engage with each other in space, they need to develop their physical memory of where they are in relation to space and each other. The following exercise gets everyone thinking visually and spatially. When it is repeated with only eye contact you gain a valuable basis for mapping work.

Entering the room 1

Ask everyone to leave the rehearsal room and re-enact exactly how they came into it for this session, following the same people, walking the same way, saying the same things.

In this replay of entering the room everyone needs to be exact:

- Who did you follow?

- What did you say?

- How did you walk?

- Where did you go?

- What did you do with your coat/bag, etc.?

After the initial chaos and corrections – in other words, once everyone has managed to render a reasonably accurate version of the group's entry – this usually provokes interesting discussion and observations. How convincing was each individual reaction to the space once they'd opened the door? Did people 'act' coming into the room or did they succeed in reprising their earlier entrance accurately? What distances did players leave between each other? If they are new to each other, distances may be greater than between those who already know each other.

Entering the room 2

Now repeat the exercise but without any speech, allowing only eye contact and gesture to indicate when individuals speak to each other. By all means split a larger group in half – those who entered first and those who kept up the rear – so players can watch each other.

As observers, be very interested in identifying where people's eyes settle and how they deport themselves in relation to the space around them and between them. You begin to see how relationships emerge in the dynamic of the space between them.

This exercise is an attempt to capture a very simple activity in order to demonstrate that the ability to recreate physical reactions to the space and each other is what conveys any sense of 'truth'. Players may find it quite challenging to replicate the initial entry; while it stands as a useful metaphor for the idea of rehearsing-as-practice, it also lays a foundation for understanding how relationships in a space are read, how visual and kinaesthetic elements create meaning for anyone watching. Taking any spoken words away puts the focus on the physical and visual.

'Actors in a theatre space can also manipulate and use the space to create meaning.'[103]

Catherine Alexander

The way players inhabit and energise space and how they activate it is a primary factor in generating meaning(s). From large-scale movements to the slightest gesture or glance, physical actions articulate what is happening to project meaning that is processed by an audience.

Whether or not you have worked on use of space previously, preliminary exploration of the space in which you are working is invaluable. In larger spaces, it is often easier to generate bigger gestures and vocal projection, but perhaps harder to convey intimacy; in smaller spaces it's vice versa. Low ceilings tend to limit and inhibit expression so try to avoid them when choosing a rehearsal space. Wherever you end up, get players to familiarise themselves with the room. The following few exercises are designed to activate and sharpen awareness of space and develop a sense of how relationships on stage can be defined by space. [NB. The first exercise is a modified version of one called *Controlling the space* from *Through the Body*, and you may also find the work on *Fixed points* from that book useful for developing spatial awareness.]

Exploring the room

This exercise should be undertaken once players have completed a warm-up for the body. Don't rush it.

Step 1

Start by lying on the floor and simply notice how you feel in the room. Notice where you are in relation to its centre and edges, how much air there is between you and the ceiling. Then close your eyes and become aware of the floor supporting you, its texture and temperature.

Step 2

Still with closed eyes, spread your arms and legs out to feel the surface beneath them. Then imagine yourself lying at the centre of the room (whether you are near it or not) and notice the feeling this prompts, and then imagine lying on the periphery.

Step 3

From this point try to imagine yourself standing on the periphery, and then standing at the centre, with your arms out wide.

Once you have taken mental note of the feelings this generates in you, bring your arms back to their sides, open your eyes, and reflect on any difference in how you feel in the room now.

Step 4

Everyone stands and takes a considered look at the floor first, then each of the walls, and finally the ceiling, turning where necessary to take in the full extent of the space.

This will invariably demonstrate a revised awareness of the space with the result that, in many cases, the room seems bigger. This is the space players will transform to create atmospheres, environments and locations. Resist the temptation to use any items of furniture, even if these are designated in the script you will be working on. Start with nothing but an empty space.

Animated space

Invite a player simply to run across the space and those watching to consider it as a moment in a play.

Immediately some kind of world is established in that one action. Watching, you might be prompted to think about who s/he might be, what or where s/he is running from or to. Whatever the image suggests, it is common for spectators to begin searching for meaning. If you subsequently invite the same player to cross the stage from the opposite direction – but slowly this time – those watching may begin making connections between the previous actions and this one. Note how changing the pace has an effect on the ways they link the two images. Is there a difference in crossing from left to right, or vice versa?

Inviting someone new to cross the space will add another layer. Are they also going from/to or are they chasing number one, perhaps? Might they even know the previous person?

What occurs after the first action is seen in relation to it. In other words, you have established what David Lan calls the 'terms of reference' for a stage-play world. He points out that when theatre-makers are figuring out how to control the meaning transmitted, they work by contrasting things.[104] Bear this in mind.

Our contact with the outside world is via the body; nerve systems, muscles and joints are an information network. How we operate in space is called the proprioceptive sense. This is the sense of your own physical self as a spatial object. It is permanently switched on, monitoring and interpreting what is around us in everyday activity, like a silent satnav. Signals from the body work with the sensors of the inner ear and the eyes, keeping us constantly informed of where we are in space and our distance from other objects and people. In everyday activity we are unaware of it, but sharpening this sense is vital to stage work, so games and exercises designed to foster it are hugely beneficial.

We tend to take space for granted, almost forgetting it's there, when in fact it is not simply 'there'. You need to consider your relationship to space before anything else if you are to truly inhabit it. And only when you truly inhabit the space can you begin to convey a sense of place and any relationship on stage.

> *'Space is not merely "there". It must be inhabited by actors and so they must think about the space they are in before anything else.'*[105]
>
> Robert Wilson

How you inhabit the space, whether there's anything in it or not, determines how an audience know where you are. Imaginative belief carries conviction; embodying an environment enables the transformation of the space in the eyes of the audience. Using only bodies and imagination to conjure a world on an empty stage invites them to invest their imaginations, and together a sense of place is established. The key to this is to play the environment rather than carting furniture on and off. The following exercise puts this into practice.

Big room/small room

Set up a couple of chairs to mark a doorway facing the audience. Players enter one at a time through the 'door', and those watching guess whether the person is coming into a big room or a small room.

To convey entering a big room, lean back to create more space in front of you and little or no space behind you; breathe in and allow your eyes to take in the imaginary walls of the room, perhaps sweeping the expanse of floor. Rotating your head will assist in this.

To convey entering a small room, you need to imagine a big space behind you and a small space in front. Your breathing changes and eye movement can take in the room and settle at a limited distance rather than rotating the head.

Once players have succeeded in convincing spectators where they are, you can play with creating more subtle distinctions, for example, moving from a house into a garden, or from an en-suite bathroom into a hotel room, and experimenting in partnership with others to develop a shared sense of where you are that communicates to others effectively. The 'trick' is a combination of imagining 'big/small' and where you settle your eyes as you enter the space.

Watching players present their work increases your awareness of how audiences respond, and you see how easy it is for one individual to shatter an illusion created by others on stage. If you see this happen, make a mental note not to repeat the error and adjust your own contribution accordingly.

By all means make a game out of this exercise, with groups creating one of the locations in the play you are working on and asking others to guess where they are. But bear in mind that playing the environment and creating the world of a play is not merely about creating illusions of realistic places. The action of running across the stage established that. The world of a play does not reside purely in its locations as places, although a play's locations inform what happens and affect characters' behaviour. *Woyzeck* is an illustration of a fractured play in fractured places with a fractured protagonist at its centre. Enclosed spaces like the Captain's washroom, the barracks and Marie's bedroom all exert pressures; out in open country Woyzeck's true nature erupts. Different places demand different energies, suggest different atmospheres, different social and interpersonal rituals.

'The type of environment it depicts, is so sharply drawn that individuals' actions are given a distinct context.'[106]

Simon Reade

The practicalities of creating a physical world are one thing. Physical place and physical time coexist. Any alternations between indoors/outdoors, enclosed/ open, domestic/

public are part and parcel of the whole. Contrasts between places, and the shifting atmosphere generated by juxtapositions between them, are structural elements. Pinning up a list of locations on the wall in the order in which they occur ensures everyone is aware of how one follows another. What do they tell you about the play, and does the order in which they occur alert you to anything more?

The rhythm of alternating locations is a structural device that has an impact on the meaning of a whole play. The restaurant in Act One of *Top Girls* establishes a public space – albeit a surreal one, populated by characters from different historical periods – before we move into the professional spheres of Marlene's workplace and the domestic sphere of Joyce and Angie's home in Acts Two and Three. The enclosed and inward-looking world of the upper classes is underlined by the house-and-garden locations of *The Importance of Being Earnest*, where the move between city and country offers little by way of contrast, indicating that these people behave rather similarly in both. Mother Courage roams the war-torn countryside of Europe hauling her cart home behind her throughout Brecht's play, and her story ends as it began with her pulling the same cart to yet another destination; although the war has finally ended and she has lost her three children, she has not changed. The street outside and the privacy of the Carbone's apartment operate simultaneously with Alfieri's office in Miller's *A View from the Bridge*, creating the world of the Brooklyn dockside and mirroring the relentlessness exerted by the Greek dramatic concept of unity of time and place, even though the time span of the play is longer than a day. When the neighbourhood crowd gather to watch the fight between Eddie and Marco, it is the community Eddie has betrayed who pour out onto the public street.

The whole of *Hamlet* takes place in the castle and its surrounding environs. The only outside scenes are those on the battlements and in the graveyard. The idea of surveillance

> 'The inner concerns of a play are revealed by its geography and by its spatial shifts.'[107]
>
> Steve Waters

permeates the play. Everyone is watching everyone else and spying is de rigueur. The BBC televised a version of the play with David Tennant in the title role (available on DVD) that was based on the RSC production and more or less transported the staging concept into a derelict building, including a highly polished black floor which mirrored the action. A key aspect of the design was the perennial presence of surveillance cameras, like those we see around us all the time, lurking in corners. In this filmed version, the action could travel to different parts of the building, such as the stairs and corridors, and to a piece of wasteland outside for the graveyard scene. This notion of travelling through a building captured the essence of the play's movement through the castle.

'Actors act as orchestra, both physically and psychically.'[108]

Steven Berkoff

By contrast, Steven Berkoff's production of *Hamlet* used a simple rectangle around which ten performers sat on forty chairs – basically an empty space. They doubled parts, playing thirty or so characters, also acting as a silent chorus, onlookers witnessing the stage traffic and occasionally murmuring to each other in response to what was happening: 'They change like chameleons, or sometimes become a mirror for the events in the centre.'[109] The surveillance here was embodied in their presence. The chorus also vocalised atmospheric elements, like the wind through the castle turrets, and, along with intermittent drumming, they created a soundscape to evoke the environments and punctuate the action. This idea of an aural dimension to the world of a play was also apparent in Cheek by Jowl's *Macbeth*, which used a similar, bare-boarded set, with actors on stage throughout, drumming their fingers when it rained. They conjured witches vocally by whispering, cajoling, and howling the fantasies in Macbeth's head. Stage blood was absent visually but represented by scraping violin strings.

The pared-down aesthetic of both these productions illustrates how Shakespeare's settings provide endless imaginative possibilities for working with an empty space. The heightened form and language of the plays, combined with our historical distance from them, induce enormous variety in the ways they are approached. Brook's 1970 production of *A Midsummer Night's Dream*, with its stark-white box set and the agility of the actors in using acrobatics and objects to evoke the world of the woods outside Athens, is a prime example. Gregory

Doran's production of the same play deployed a puppet for the changeling boy Oberon and Titania argue over, with dolls as puppets for the fairies. Plays with more realistic or specific scenic requirements do not immediately provoke the kind of creative solutions that arise from these plays. All too often, once you put a table and chairs on stage, the constraints of naturalistic thinking creep in.

It is easy to get hung up on the idea that you have to start by portraying location to create the illusion of characters in a particular place. However, if you start thinking realistically too early, you may jeopardise a

'Becoming the environment releases in the actor the total possibilities of their creative potential.'[110]

Steven Berkoff

group's ability to work more imaginatively in space. The world of a play is not simply where things happen; it is something less tangible, more complex. When things are presented too literally, they are robbed of their poetry. Theatre is fundamentally a metaphorical medium. The hotel room in Sarah Kane's *Blasted* should be familiar and anodyne like hotel rooms everywhere; the explosion and the arrival of the soldier bring the uncomfortable truth of war into the ostensible comfort of those surroundings.

'Learning the language of space gives the theatre-maker an endless number of possibilities.'[111]

Catherine Alexander

Whatever play you are working on, the exercises that follow open up less prosaic and literal ways of working, and encourage players to explore the concept of transforming the space. The earlier exercise of *Big room/small room* tends to encourage literal thinking and representations of recognisable places; the next one adapts it to create more abstract realms and find the metaphorical dimensions of space, moving towards the realm of the grotesque.

Huge and tiny

Use the earlier exercise of *Big room/small room,* but here the fun comes from magnifying and decreasing size, exploding it to massive proportions or constricting it to miniscule ones. Group sizes here should be between five and seven.

Invite groups to create a sense of vast spaces or landscapes such as a football stadium or a range of mountains. Use the maximum dimensions of the room you rehearse in, using windowsills and open doors or clambering over any bulky items.

Contrast this space by creating a tiny one like a pothole or drawer, even with up to seven in a group. Squeezing several players into a tiny space immediately provokes hilarity. Larger environments require imaginative use of spatial dynamics, and the bigger the space the bigger the gestures have to be.

Once the diametrically different environments are established, repeat them in succession, alternating between absolutely massive and minute.

As you 'play' each one, find a moment of stillness in which each player conveys through whole bodily gesture their pleasure or glee, frustration or anxiety at being there and communicate this to those watching. Let this be prompted by simply the awkward position you find yourselves in or the expanse around you. Don't make up or 'act' emotions: use the feeling you have in the space and exaggerate that.

Noise is a good accompaniment. Avoid actual words and go for sounds that accentuate and express the way breath is being inhaled and exhaled in each environment. Making connections between what you do and breathing is such a fruitful route into physicality, and something to return to often. Limiting the sounds to only those that can be made with mouths closed makes players focus more on using their eyes in communicating the emotional dimension. And once again, as with the *Entering the room 2* exercise, you begin to realise how important looks between players and clocking the audience are in communication on and from a stage.

Moving directly from these exercises to tackling the setting of plays with ostensibly realistic settings opens up players to using space in more inventive ways. When players engage in creating those environments

> '*What you're aiming to evoke at this stage is the world of the play, its aura, almost its force field.*'[112]
>
> Simon Callow

immediately following the *Huge and tiny* exercise, they are more likely to approach the task with the idea of transforming space, placing individuals in relation to any furniture items in innovative ways and disregarding the need for verisimilitude: 'playing against the realistic space can make a piece much more theatrical'.[113] One group in a workshop of mine chose to mime the idea of larger-than-life furniture in the interior scenes of *Saved*; as they worked through an improvised run of key points identified in those domestic locations, this made the surroundings seem to weigh down on the characters, giving an impression of their insignificance in relation to society at large. The group had summed up the world of the play in this exercise, and although one might not choose to present it in that particular style in a production, the ideas enhanced their understanding of the play.

The world of a play is much more than simply places. The environments in which events occur may seem realistic on the surface, but exploring these and the contrasts between them makes mapping a play more than simply identifying a series of locations. With actors in an empty space you can be anywhere, nowhere and everywhere in the blink of an eye. The physical world is an environment encompassing thematic and metaphorical connotations. As such it is as much a tool in telling stories on stage as are the scripted words. It is space – space that can be transformed.

> '*To be able to evoke another world through the simplest of means is not only marvellous, but, I think, part of the meaning of theatre.*'[114]
>
> Simon McBurney

Complicite's work revels in imaginative play; their ability to transform space underpins the quality they exude on stage, giving their work a markedly spatial eloquence. The company often work with bamboo canes – straight garden canes six feet in length – and these became integral to their production of *The Caucasian Chalk Circle*, used both to define smaller places on stage and to create the bridge Grusha crosses with the baby. But they do not use them only to create physical spaces. In workshops, using bamboos is also a powerful way of exploring how space and movement can express meaningful emotions and atmospheres. This next exercise helps to create a sense of the dynamic relationship between performers in space.

You need a big space for this exercise if you have a large group. Once you get to the stage of experimenting in smaller groups, reduce the numbers playing and let others observe, then swap over.

Space dynamics[115]

Each player holds their bamboo cane vertically, ten centimetres off the ground.

Players move around the space, without bumping into each other, keeping their canes upright and the same distance from the ground. Being precise is part of the fun.

In groups of three, continue moving together as one. Then change leader with each change of direction whilst keeping close together.

Once you find the necessary concentration to move well together, begin experimenting with different speeds, and trying different configurations – three abreast, single file, triangle – as well as altering the distance between your canes.

It is important to keep the ideas and movements simple and precise. It is the togetherness of groups moving the bamboos exactly as one which is most effective.

'Players have to be able to place themselves with reference to others, in a clear relationship of listening and response.'[116]

Jacques Lecoq

As you watch, see which ideas work best. Some may inspire you to use bamboos in creating environments, although that is not the main purpose. The benefit lies in the impact it has on players' imaginative use of space, in establishing spatial relationships and in keeping the space alive. Like the next exercise, it is one to return to at various points during a rehearsal process as a reminder of the need to invest in the quality of space.

The value of 'stage balancing' lies in establishing spatial awareness in respect of bodies on stage. You need a minimum of five, and it works well with groups of up to twelve.

Stage balancing

Set the parameters of the stage area as a square with players placed on all four sides.

Imagine the stage area is resting on a huge ball situated underneath in the centre. As one player enters the stage area the floor will tip with their weight. The task of the next player is to counteract the weight of the first person with their own to keep the stage level. Movement from either player forces the other to move in counterbalance.

This game can be developed to allow one player against several.

This is an exercise to return to and play when establishing the choreography of movement in a scene where there are several entrances and exits. As each new character enters, everyone on stage has to re-negotiate their relationship to the space and to each other in a way that balances the stage, even at the most subtle of levels. It is also invaluable for chorus work, where balancing the stage becomes an integral dimension of a play such as *Antigone*, with characters pitted against each other.

Mapping: action

Mapping the action begins with the whole company sketching out ideas for movement through whole play, pooling ideas as they go before they get into any intellectual discussion. It is in effect creating a scenario, paring down the action in a similar way to how a dramatist outlines the events of a play in the sequence in which the story will unfold. Non-verbal improvisation work like this is a great starting point for 'choreographing the knowledge', getting to grips with narrative, forcing players to find visual means of conveying information. Enjoy the roughness of this early work. Roughness and simplicity are staging posts in the search for clarity.

The only assumption made from here on is that players will have individually already read the play you're working on; keep texts in the room to consult when necessary. There is no need to decide on casting at this point; if you need characters at any points draw the names from a hat.

'We make a version to tell the story in a first draft purely visually with no words. It isn't about having good ideas, they will come once you find the story clearly.'[117]

Paul Hunter

This is where you begin 'choreographing the knowledge'. While a dramatist writes their scenario in prose, film-makers use storyboarding to sketch out how scenes will look pictorially, resulting in a physical score where characters are placed very precisely in order to illustrate the action. The notion of 'storyboarding' is valuable as long as you realise this is achieved through collaboration, and is not meant to be a way of 'fixing' actions by literary analysis. To divorce himself from the literary nature of a drama, the theatre-maker and director Robert Wilson uses the text as a springboard, creating a 'visual-book' where he records annotated drawings and suggestions as he responds to retellings of the source text from his team.

You need a really secure shared familiarity with the story of the play before you can begin interpreting it in any way. *Twitterature* is a little book that attempts to capture the essence of some of the 'great classics' of Western literature, each in a couple of pages of 'tweets'. This tongue-in-cheek enterprise may be frowned upon by literary academics, but it points up the fact that once you know the story well enough, it can be broken into bite-sized pieces. The one for *Macbeth* has nineteen tweets from the central character's viewpoint – @Big-MAC – and his final tweet reads: 'Shit. "C-section" is not "of woman born"? What kind of king dies on a goddamn technicality?'[118] With Shakespeare, getting to know the story of the play can be challenging for those unfamiliar with the poetic language. Reading a synopsis before reading the play for the first time is not cheating but helpful. And playing with tweets to accompany images makes analysis fun.

Five-point flash-play 1

Assuming everyone has read the play and absorbed the gist of it, put the texts to one side and use them for reference if necessary.

Step 1

Working in small groups, decide on five significant incidents from the play. Select those vital to the whole because you reckon something happens to change the situation; you are looking for moments around which others derive meaning and significance.

Allow some quick-fire discussion about which incidents are most salient, but limit the amount of time – three minutes is about right – as this will force players to deal with essentials.

Step 2

Each group creates five dynamic moving images of up to ten seconds duration capturing the incidents chosen. These should be energised moments caught as though in the midst of action occurring in 3D on the stage rather than framed photographic stills. Allow the understanding gained through playing the stage-balancing game to inform the ideas to allow relationships between characters and space and the amount of space between the characters to convey the actions. Once again, limit the time allowed – three minutes – as this really focuses the work.

There is no need to embellish anything with complicated props; find solutions from using players' bodies or by using anything lying around in the rehearsal room. Encourage players to interact dynamically, using their awareness of spatial dynamics, for example, Ismene might be trying to pull Antigone across the space as the first image of Sophocles' play. There is no need for any dialogue, keep the focus on the action.

Share these flash-plays with groups watching each other. As each flash-play is presented a sense of the story will start to emerge; at this stage that is all you're looking for. Since stories work on different levels, groups are likely to choose different incidents, some will work out emotional journeys and others concentrate more on action. There is no right or wrong choice, though decisions made by players can be teased out in discussion. Relish the way variances provoke debate, developing a familiarity with the play as you search for clarity. What are the points of contact between the different versions in terms of content and/or style and use of space? Which ideas seem exciting and theatrical and which seem to fall back on more mundane approaches? Are any of the ideas striking or unusual? The most important question will ultimately be 'how well did they tell the story?'

Some plays have a more pronounced sense of progression than others. Usually this is due to the relative importance of plot; in plays driven by a linear cause-and-effect narrative where the actions of a central protagonist provoke consequences, logical progression is more evident. Like mainstream films, the story in such plays is usually kick-started by one incident, often called the 'inciting incident'. So, for example, Antigone's decision to bury her brother against King Creon's edict sets in motion a chain of events which show the consequences of her actions unravelling. In this play that first incident is a key action point – the rest of the story depends on it. The inciting incident is not always as clear as this, and since stories work on different levels, there may be variety in the choice of the key points.

> 'An actor's job is to do the story and be the story.'[119]
>
> Willem Dafoe

> 'We treat the source as a story and find narrative in the landscape of the text.'[120]
>
> Emma Rice

Five-point flash-play 2

Take the same five points identified by your group in the previous exercise but this time focus on creating these five moments purely through a soundscape.

Using just vocal and percussive sounds, convey the same story of the five points of action in a sound-only improvisation. This is non-verbal work, so do not use words, only vocalisation and sound effects – including silence. Sounds can be made by drumming fingers, clapping, hitting your body in different places, or banging items of furniture – anything lying around.

Here you are less concerned with literal visual or physical representation of the narrative points as you search for sounds to convey the underbelly of the action. They give a sense of the underlying tensions and feelings between characters and their relationship to events.

By this stage everyone should have a better acquaintance with key events and gained some confidence in how the play progresses, while also developing ideas for lively visual stage imagery. Even if there is no apparent story as such, it is important to establish images that capture the chain of events and the order in which they occur. Moving on to presenting improvised versions of the whole play in the next exercise will show how much has been grasped and how imagery and movement are emerging. The aim of this is to develop an active approach to visual storytelling. You are aiming for immediacy, simplicity, focus. We are all familiar with film trailers that sum up a new film in a series of fast-flowing images designed to entice us back to see the whole film – this is similar.

Ten-point trailers

Allow time for groups to reflect on the previous work they have created – both their own and from watching others – and to expand five points from the flash-plays into ten points. These ten points create a two- to three-minute version of the whole play which integrates action-imagery with a soundscape, utilising and extending the material developed in the last two exercises.

Be clear about moments where actions and/or sounds are punctuated by a pause, whether this is within a moment or in between events.

These trailers outline the play in broad strokes. A valuable ploy to make the shared understanding of the story more concrete at this stage, is to play a game of Keepy-uppy, where players try and keep a ball or balloon up in the air by patting it between them, while telling the story verbally. The first player begins the story and the rest continue while also focusing on keeping the balloon airborne. As soon as the balloon hits the floor, you need to start telling from the beginning. It is very frustrating initially as players tend to tell too much of the story, often very descriptively. They get better at condensing the story when they find that the more gently they tap the balloon between them, the more they listen to each other and track the flow of the story. This can be used as part of subsequent warm-ups to keep clarifying the story before rehearsals.

> *'There's a "superstructure", the rhythm of the whole. Working on this at the start means it's easier to adjust later on, finding points where a little more pace or a longer beat will serve the story.'*[121]
>
> Emma Rice

Mapping: theme

Just as crucial as a shared purchase on story is a shared understanding of the central themes. Gathering ideas and personal responses about a play is similar to creative devising methods where plastering the rehearsal space with images, newspaper stories, poems and photographs spur creative work. Encourage players to draw or write lyrics or poems. If you are not always working in the same space, make 'mood boards' with the materials so they can be transported, or borrow Robert Wilson's idea of a visual book and create a rehearsal sketchpad crammed with scribbled ideas as well as drawings, or a box of material that can be stored and retrieved when work restarts.

Creative research is essential whether you have chosen a play, or are working with one chosen for you. The crucial thing is what you do with it. Sharing findings is a way of connecting to thematic material on common ground and reinforces the collaborative nature of the work. This way of working is absolutely central to companies who value collaboration, creating installations with their findings and creative writings. Presenting ideas orally and reading aloud encourages players to really connect with the material and each other. Annie Castledine's directing valued 'the whole company exploring every problem through improvisation and exercises'.[122]

'Expect every actor to do a lot of research, not just on their part but on the play. Research is a useful tool for freeing the actor's imagination.'[123]

Declan Donnellan

Improvising with themes is a vital avenue, often serving to capture more abstract dimensions and generate potent imagery. The themes of classic plays from the past often seem distant to us. To discover contemporary relevance does not necessarily mean modernising a play, but simply seeing similarities between your society and that of a play. For the original Greek audience, *Antigone* concerned the conflict between religious law and state law, a conflict apparent in societies where religion is allied with government. Versions and adaptations of this play frequently draw parallels with modern war, such as those by Brecht and Anouilh which relate to the Second World War. Tom Paulin's 1980s re-visioning is set in Belfast during the Troubles; called *The Riot Act*, the conflict in his version is always a one-sided debate, with Creon as a brutally voiced Unionist and Antigone as his Republican adversary. The debate is less directly partisan in Seamus Heaney's tautly poetic rendering of Sophocles' play in translation, although it is perhaps worth noting that his version called *The Burial at Thebes* was written during the 2003 Iraq War. The word 'burial' sums up the central concern for any audience since almost all cultures hold a deep respect for burying their dead (whether or not the body is actually laid under earth), and that one word provides a fertile starting point for creative research to feed improvisation. Researching rituals and religious laws governing funeral rites in differing cultures throws up many parallels, as well as providing concrete images for physical improvisation and exploration not tied to the particular conflicts of Sophocles' play.

Before the next exercise, you need to identify the themes in the play you are working on.

Mini-mapping: themes

Groups should remain at between five and seven players but no one is allowed to move outside a defined area of not more than 1.5m by 2.5m. Players work through any of the themes identified in the play on this mini-stage.

When you find several themes operating in the play, invite groups to choose one and work it through the whole play rather than trying to accommodate all of them in one exercise.

This mini-mapping forces decisions to be made through the limitation of working in a small space, but gets to the root of what is going on thematically and how this functions throughout the play. It is perfectly normal for players to feel insecure when this is suggested. Ignore any doubts. Ideas that surface are always worth exploring. Questions raised through this work become routes to making decisions about a play. If a theme appears to become redundant at any point, that flags up further investigation. What is happening when a theme appears to be dropped or seems irrelevant at any point in the play? What is happening when one theme dominates? What happens when an individual scene or section of a play seems inundated with a theme? Do all the characters present aspects of it? How does the theme relate to the world of the play in terms of environment?

An example of how this works is from a workshop on *Top Girls* where players created two powerful images. One was of a woman raised above the heads of other players with her hands clawing towards the ceiling as they ignored her and shuffled round underneath her; the other was a woman hanging on to a door handle (the group had defined their area near a door) while the other players tried to tug her away. Like the image of characters in *Saved* hemmed in by imaginary outsized furniture, these images demonstrate a forceful level of practical engagement with the themes of the play.

Serious playful improvisational work can get to the heart of a play to generate understanding, though sometimes a plethora of imagery and associations can

'If you're lucky, five per cent of what you create has life and the rest is rejected.'[124]

Catherine Alexander

threaten to drown the play itself. Recognising how creative exploration throws up masses of material is part and parcel of the process. It is not about looking for final solutions for a performance at this stage but opening up possibilities. The importance of allowing exploratory time to travel into a play's hinterland cannot be overstated, but accepting that much of what you actually create will end up on your 'cutting-room floor' is crucial to pursuing a really productive process.

Before collectively reading the play, try the *Route map* exercise that follows. The aim of this is to create snapshots of the traffic onstage during the course of a play, as though a time-lapse camera has been in operation. It reveals a skeleton outline to which you can return at various points in the rehearsal process, each time adding new layers of understanding. Although it resembles what used to be called a 'French scene', where stage managers plotted the entrances and exits, it is more akin to an 'animatic', where animators show a rough sketch of a cartoon or animated film moving through key images. By this time, players have an informed sense of working in space, a clear grasp of the story of the play and have engaged with its world and the underlying themes it embodies.

Route map

Assign someone the task of being 'Caller'.

Set up the space with a large horseshoe shape marked out on the floor to represent the stage; players stand around the curved perimeter (this is to avoid ending up with a series of framed pictures instead of three-dimensional images that exploit the use of stage space). Allocate characters by drawing the names out of a hat, including all those with relatively few lines and any who are non-speaking. If working in a small group, work out necessary doublings. If working in a large group, assign pairs or trios of players to share the presentation of characters, taking it in turns to play them in different scenes.

The Caller calls out the act, scene and cue line for every individual entrance and exit, stating which characters come on and go off. Players come on and go off accordingly. Although you want this to happen speedily, they can show by their demeanour or physical attitude to other characters what is happening at this point in the play.

You will need to persevere with this exercise with large-cast plays, such as *A Midsummer Night's Dream*, as chaos can ensue. It often demonstrates initially that players don't really know who's who or what's going on during the first attempt. In *A Midsummer Night's Dream* the contrast between scenes in the forest compared with the formality of the court scenes and those of the mechanicals soon becomes apparent, and players start to become aware of how the different plots are interwoven in overlapping sequences.

Several notable points emerge from using this exercise with a Shakespeare play:

- The way characters move so swiftly from place to place.

- The placing of private scenes between a few pairs of characters in contrast to highly populated scenes.

- The fact that rarely does a character ending one scene begin the next.

- The arrival of characters appearing only once (such as the Third Murderer who joins in the attempt on Banquo and Fleance in *Macbeth*) which can flag up plot points that require attention.

Just as changes of location are aspects of structure, so are entrances and exits. Navigating your way through a play like this is a way of surveying the whole play. Greek tragedies were essentially one-act plays, with tension sustained by continuous action in a single place. The drama would have been played on a stage with little scenic furnishing. The action of *Antigone* happens outside the Palace of Thebes. Offstage one way leads to the Palace, offstage in another direction leads to the battlegrounds beyond the city and the hill where Polynices's body is exposed. This immediately indicates entrances and exits: Creon emerging and disappearing always into the Palace, the Messenger arriving from outside the city. In this example it is fairly straightforward to sketch in the whole play jumping from entrances to exits, and the significance of the chorus remaining onstage throughout is clear from the outset.

Other plays do not have such clear staging embodied in them. But it is worth noting the points at which the stage is full and when it is almost empty or even actually empty, as such moments have a kinaesthetic effect on the spectator. There is a pleasure in seeing a stage fully populated, while a character alone attracts a different curiosity. The physical rhythms of a play become apparent, creating a preliminary sense of how the ebb and flow of the structure will become manifest in performing the whole.

Once players get the hang of this exercise – and it can take several goes, so it is one to keep trying at various points – they begin to grasp the dynamic inherent in a play's flow, noticing where contrasts occur between short and long scenes, those with few characters, and scenes where traffic is virtually continuous. Individual scenes with many comings and goings are highlighted alongside those moments where a character is alone on stage. The almost continuous presence of one character, which occurs in *Woyzeck* and *Mother Courage and Her Children*, for example, reveals the centrality of their role. Players can discern key pointers to theatrical style: the fact that the chorus remain for the duration of the play once they arrive is patently obvious with *Antigone* as with Berkoff's *Greek*. The presence of Eddie's neighbours and co-workers on occasion in *A View from the Bridge* indicates not only the context of the Brooklyn community but the chorus-like nature of their role, expanded when the whole community watches the fight at the end; when characters for the next 'scene' appear before the last one has finished in this play you sense its wave-like rhythm. The few entrances and exits in *Waiting for Godot* become significant precisely because there are so few of them. A very different atmosphere comes with the measured plotting of Bond's *Saved*, where the audience work out what has occurred between scenes as each one unfolds. In *Top Girls*, the way the rhythm of the first act is punctuated by the toing and froing of the waitress becomes apparent, and the moment when Angie enters in the final image registers its significance.

Replaying the *Route map* with the *Trailer plays* inserted at the point where they occur illustrates the placing of key incidents in relation to the rest of the play. The arrangement of incidents constitutes the plot; the placing of these creates a pattern, demonstrating that the playwright has chosen where each incident is placed in relation to others and how long it lasts. The timing of events is therefore a factor in understanding the play and its potential effects.

Readthrough

A readthrough is an audible map with everyone listening collectively to the play. Directors frequently conduct readthroughs with no one reading the part in which they have been cast: Deborah Warner, Katie Mitchell and Gregory Doran have all done so. Waiting until players have already engaged in work on the play as a whole before having a readthrough means the opportunity to read a variety of parts gives everyone a more objective view and they share their discoveries of the play from the start. Hearing different voices in the room reading different parts provides insights into how each character serves the play.

In a collaborative ensemble all the performers are at all rehearsals for the duration of the rehearsal period. Players get involved in trying out moments in the play and sharing discoveries with a whole company exploring all the problems through improvisation and exercises. As Nancy Meckler says, 'it's always about collaboration and the really theatrical ideas coming right off the floor.'[126]

'If you read different parts you get a purchase on how important some characters are to other characters.'[125]

Jane Hartley

The journeys characters make through a play are what concerns the next section.

Section 4

Charting the Journeys

Charting the Journeys

While geographical maps show the lie of the land, charts, like those used in nautical navigation, indicate the depths. While work on mapping connects you with a play's flow – how the narrative unfolds, how relationships develop and moods shift – charting the journeys of characters as they progress through the play registers their relationships in and to the whole play, enabling you to note key points of significance as they unfold with the story, where they are changed, or change tack. These first impressions will be qualified as rehearsals move on, which is as it will be for an audience too – only by the end of the performance is the true complexity of a character revealed. By the end of the play characters are in a different place; monitoring what they do to develop a connecting thread from the beginning to the end outlines the arc of their stories.

'For the audience, they [characters] are no more nor less than the sum of their actions.'[127]

Steve Waters

The idea of surprise in relation to character is critical. They are not fixed identities; any attempt to pin them down through singular meaning is futile. Just as in life we are a bundle of conflicting selves jostling for attention and presenting different selves in different contexts, characters present different facets in different situations and with different characters, and it's easy to forget they are fictional constructs when we talk about them as though they exist as living beings. Let them continue to surprise you. However intriguing or fascinating or repulsive they are, they are figments of a dramatist's imagination. And, whatever the pleasure in their creation, for the dramatist their role in the play starts at a functional level: they enact the plot.

Plots move characters through changes, shifting them from point to point and back again, sometimes gradually, sometimes remarkably quickly. Shakespeare is a case in point. His characters can switch between one state and another with alarming alacrity: 'mad with joy in one line, mad with grief the next, the human being is there in all its entirety in each succeeding instant.'[128] Changes in other plays occur at a less frenetic pace. Where characters end up is the measure of how they have changed. Even those who appear unchanged by the end of the play have travelled in order to return to their earlier equilibrium.

Delaying final casting decisions until everyone has a shared investment in the story allows you to explore characters fully as a group. Casting too early often means you resort to casting by type, or make assumptions about characters without the benefit of discoveries to be made during exploratory work. And these explorations can usefully happen before dialogue is embedded. If lines are learnt prior to rehearsals there is the danger of developing individual isolated approaches to action and choices about characters. Decisions locked down too early straitjacket interpretation. Learning in conjunction with exploring the text collaboratively, discovering impulses through active partnerships to allow what lies behind the words to become manifest, gives meaning and style more room to develop as players evolve with the play.

Even when casting is in place, line-learning is not always undertaken by professional actors before rehearsals: Mark Rylance goes in and experiments with the play in his own words until he eventually arrives at the actual script, and Harriet Walter warns how learning lines prior to rehearsals means 'there is a danger of rigidity setting in. Tunes get in the brain and are hard to scrub out. If you prematurely lock into one interpretation while working in isolation, you may miss something more interesting that comes out in rehearsal'.[130] In an interview about playing Hamlet, David Tennant revealed that he didn't start learning his lines until

> '*It is in muscular memory that the learning of a part takes place.*'[129]
>
> John Harrop

after the first day of rehearsals because once committed to memory the brain inevitably 'remembers them as part of an emotional journey'.[131] A character does not exist in isolation. Each is defined by their actions and the choices they make in relation to situations they face and those around them.

Tackling a readthrough on your feet, like the cast in Complicite's production of *Measure for Measure* at the National Theatre, reinforces the place of every character in relation to the whole in an active and tangible manner. In a stand-up readthrough, players are less likely to feel they need to 'act' or read with inflections based on decisions about a character. It forces really listening to one another and hearing the words; you gain a more objective sense of the play as a result. Cast the play by drawing names from a hat, including all non-speaking parts and those who have few lines, as you did for the *Route map* exercise in the previous section, so no one reads their 'own' part.

Stand-up readthrough

Set up the space with two lines – one at the back of the stage and one at the front. Those in the first scene stand on the back line – any order will do at this point. As each enters the scene they come forward and speak directly out to the audience in a neutral fashion, remaining on the front line until the script indicates they exit.

As one scene draws to a close those in the following scene need to be ready on the back line so that there is no break between the end of a scene and the next. Include non-speaking characters in every scene.

For the stage directions, designate a player to stand alongside or just to the side of the characters and read them to the audience, including 'silences' and 'pauses', but exclude those in brackets that indicate emotional indications of delivery or another character being addressed.

Like the *Route map*, this illustrates different populations in scenes as players step forward and back, as well as contrasts between short and long scenes. It also makes everyone aware of when non-speaking characters or those who say very little are actually present in a scene.

Everyone on stage is an active participant in the proceedings, whether they contribute to what others are doing or not. They cannot be neutral since an audience will see them as making some kind of statement in relation to what's going on. While there may be one main protagonist, all characters have their own journeys through the play which may serve to draw out the various aspects of conflict inherent in her or him, or may offer a different perspective on the theme.

On a pragmatic note, if you intend to stage the play in a site-specific context, you gain a useful impression of how to divide the play into various spaces in your site. It is also invaluable for working out any necessary doubling for a production if you are a small group dealing with a large-cast play.

'The starting point is to give the character a journey through the play that is plausible and supports the story.'[132]

David Lan

The journey of characters starts with an initial state of being and moves through a series of changes as they encounter challenges. Changes a character negotiates are not always activated by themselves: they can be external, i.e. what happens beyond the character's control, such as a change of fortune, circumstance or role, or imposed by outside forces; as well as internal ones, prompted perhaps by a change of heart or mind, faith or belief, affection or a change in moral outlook in response to events or what others do or say. A character comprises a complex matrix of actions played during the course of their journey. However, at this preliminary stage it is worth simplifying and dividing them into two: the physical actions, which are the external or outward manifestation of events, such as Macbeth killing Duncan, and the internal or emotional actions, which are what goes on inside the characters as the story progresses.

What follows is a playful way to connect with this. It builds on the kind of work undertaken on the world of the play in the previous section, opening up potential for choreographing the knowledge of the play through physical imagery, as well as fostering an appreciation of the relationship between character and plot.

Obstacle course

Select one character from the play you are working on.

Groups build an obstacle course using their bodies in various configurations and/or any items lying around the rehearsal room, such as pieces of furniture large and small, waste-paper bins, canes, bags, curtains – whatever. These obstacles stand for the challenges the character encounters during the play – people, things, themselves – that threaten their desired outcome.

Make use of your five or ten points from the work on mapping if these are relevant.

Obstacles need to be sculptural to allow a player to move through them, over them or have to negotiate a way round them. Creating obstacles with extremes in differing heights and size makes the game more fun and augments the sense of moving through the play in a tangible way that carries into work on the text.

Once groups are happy with the course, players take it in turn to take on the mantle of the character and attempt to complete the course as fast as possible.

A central protagonist from a play with a conventional linear structure, like Macbeth or Antigone or Woyzeck, responds really well to this and demonstrates how structure has a particularly powerful impact when wedded to the journey of a central character. It is all too easy to let a focus on central characters dominate at the expense of other characters, who may be used as counterpoints to the central character, and neglect the individual journeys of those. Developing the game to work out contrasts between characters or explore relationships between any who have close bonds – and seeing how they tackle obstacles – throws up new patterns. Devising obstacle courses for different characters (simultaneously if you have enough space) in order to compare them is also productive. It can be more challenging but equally rewarding to create a journey for a character from less conventional structures, such as *Blasted* or *Saved*, although the route and passage often creates a less frenetic race.

'A leading role can be – must be – arranged into valleys and peaks.'[133]

Simon Callow

The active nature of struggling through the play-as-obstacle-course, whether taking on the mantle of a character or creating the physical obstacles, makes this a memorable game. Points where characters face dilemmas or turning points in the plot emerge strongly, together with a sense of how they arrive in a different place by the end of the play.

Characters – function and force

Characters do not merely inhabit a story; the story is transmitted through the choices they make: in enacting the plot, they are functions within the play's scheme, in enacting the theme they are active forces, often in conflict with each other. What they do and how they change, or not, is revealed through their actions and reactions. These actions, born of their physical independent life on the stage, express the central core and idea of the play. And in the play's situations, when characters interact and respond to events and others, we observe 'the way in which [each] person is revealed under pressure'.[134] The dramatic action is designed to reveal character to demonstrate their essential nature, their kernel if you like, moments when they, and the audience, discover – sometimes with surprise – what they actually want and how that relates to the whole.

Character and story are the proverbial chicken and egg. Story is embedded in those actions, reactions and interactions of characters to the particular situations they find themselves in. It is the dramatic

'Characters in plays are there, when it boils down to it, to perform certain tasks.'[135]

Alan Ayckbourn

need of characters that fuels the story. Playwrights create situations where characters' intentions, whether conscious or unconscious, become apparent and, once pursued, provoke consequences. The story unfolds through what they *do*. The major question to delve into at this stage is not 'who is this character?' or 'what does this character want?' but 'what is this character's function?' and 'what force do they animate?' in terms of the debate smouldering in the play. They are not simply interesting people who might be witty, ambitious or depressed, but have a *purpose* in relation to the dramatic action of the play; like cogs in a wheel they function at an operational level. Why are they there? What do they do? How do they serve the story, the theme? And does their function alter at all during the course of the play?

Lady Macbeth, for example, could be labelled a 'helper' initially as she goads her husband, sweeping his doubts aside, and when he struggles to complete the task, finishes it for him, taking the bloody daggers from his hands and returning to Duncan's chamber to smear the grooms with blood in order to implicate them. In criminal terminology she aids and abets. She is still in 'helpful' mode during the banquet scene when Macbeth is ruffled by the vision of Banquo's ghost, scurrying around to appease their guests and cover up her husband's bizarre behaviour. Yet once her husband has launched into slaughtering innocent women and children, i.e. Macduff's wife and bairns, she descends into lamenting the crime they conceived together. This is not simply pitiable; her guilt and remorse serves a new function in presenting the antithesis of Macbeth's increasing paranoid megalomania, and, since Shakespeare places her sleep-walking scene in the wake of those needless murders, the contrast has added resonance.

'The function of the character is why you're there – you're there to serve the story.'[136]

Jane Hartley

Fusing character with plot is how dramatists embody conflict. *Antigone* is a beautifully crafted play with plot, characters and theme so tightly interwoven as to be virtually seamless. The set up of Antigone and Creon is straightforwardly oppositional; they are pitted against each other to act out the central debate, forces ranged against each other from the start of the play. Ismene stands in clear contrast to her sister at the outset, opposing Antigone's proposal to bury their brother against their Uncle Creon's diktat which refuses burial rites to enemy soldiers. In Ismene's second appearance she attempts appeasement, offering to join her sister in burying their brother's body – in effect to share the transgression – but Antigone digs in her heels and refuses her help. Ismene is a foil to Antigone in terms of the debate Sophocles is dramatising. She is not merely a thorn in Antigone's side but a plot device that increases the isolation of her sister and serves to reinforce Antigone's choice of martyrdom. Antigone's fiancé and cousin Haemon complicates the plot by creating pressure on his father Creon, forcing him to face a dilemma similar to Antigone's, i.e. whether to privilege the family over state and release her as she is his niece as well as his son's wife-to-be. Yet Haemon does not appeal to his father to save Antigone for personal or family reasons; it is the citizens Haemon invokes: 'Surely she deserves to be honoured rather than condemned? That is what they are whispering' (p. 28). And, once the prophet Tiresias has endorsed Haemon's view, it is the citizens in the form of the chorus of elders whose advice Creon eventually seeks and follows, albeit too late to redeem Antigone.

Arthur Miller pits the moral law of family and community against the civil law of the state which requires its citizens to inform on illegal immigrants in *A View from the Bridge*. Like a character in a Greek tragedy turning to the chorus for solace or advice, Eddie seeks out the lawyer Alfieri, who mediates between the action on stage and the audience in a similar way to a Greek chorus, his function part-narrator/part-commentator. When Eddie then phones the Immigration Bureau to turn in Marco and Rodolpho, his action betrays not only his wife's cousins but the community in which he works and lives. This community is built into Miller's directions for the set design, which not only creates the Brooklyn dockside environment but serves the function of making visible the people Eddie betrays, for, when Marco resorts to the Sicilian law of revenge and kills Eddie in the fight at the end, they are witnesses. This example illustrates the importance of small parts (some of them interact with Eddie at various points) as well as non-speaking roles in a specific play, and how vital it is not to dismiss such roles. If the playwright has put them there, s/he has a reason.

So function is equally important with characters operating on the fringes of a play. Calling them 'minor' characters is not helpful. Despite seeming peripheral they too are there to serve the story, and you need to figure out their significance in relation to the action of the whole play at points when they are off stage as well as when on it. Are they there to create tension, or harmony, to deflect attention, to provide comic contrast, or to give a sense of the world of the play and its offstage life? Or if they have a concrete purpose in terms of the thematic concerns of the play, what force do they represent? Their presence is tangible in the *Stand-up readthrough*, signalling the need to address their purpose in concrete terms. The notion of 'spear-carrier' or 'walk-on part' is obsolete. The waitress in Act One of *Top Girls* does not merely serve the food. She is crucial to the set-up of the dinner party with Marlene from the twentieth century and the other women from other centuries and other parts of the globe, fiction and art. Without her the scene could be seen as a fantasy of Marlene's; with her there, taking orders and bringing wine and food, the surreal world appears virtually normal – she anchors the situation in a recognisable reality.

'Small parts are always crucial. They have a vital function in the narrative, they establish the social milieu. They underpin the play with their own resonances.'[137]

Simon Callow

Every character in Brecht's plays, however small the role, serves a sociopolitical function. The Armourer who barters with Mother Courage in the tiny opening unit of Scene Three demonstrates the insidious everyday reality of black-marketeering in the war. As for Yvette's Colonel, Brecht says, 'His only function is to show the price the whore must pay for her rise in life',[138] and he suggests this is a difficult role to play because it requires real invention from the player. Berkoff incorporates named characters in a chorus that has a function in stagecrafting the play's aesthetic, observing the action while also creating the environment, as in his production of *Hamlet*, or peopling the stage with cameo performances of individuals who represent a whole community, as in *Greek*.

'You don't need portrayal, you need action.'[139]

David Mamet

Getting to know characters in action means you discover their different facets through enacting incidents separately. And reasons for each individual character's actions emerge gradually. If you try pinning these down too early you are likely to lock out alternatives that have more depth. Unity eventually emerges through the accumulation of actions in the play, so that when the spectators arrive at the end of the play they appreciate the character in full.

You cannot act the play on your own. Psychological immersion in a character to the exclusion of all else can derail a play. Actors who focus on individual psychological motivation without reference to the whole or to other characters 'disappear up Psychology Lane', in the words of Mike Alfreds, and this is to be avoided. Harriet Walter advises thinking of characters in the third person for as long as possible to ensure clarity about the whole, otherwise 'actors can be sidetracked by their own psychological wallowing and the play gets becalmed.'[140] Whatever inner logic actors discern in a character needs to comply with inner logic of the play as a whole; remaining objective about characters and reserving judgement or pity are both essential. And emotions are visceral, not cerebral. Audiences can have no real relationship with characters if they are sentimentalised nor if any sense of foreboding is conveyed before a character meets a sticky end. The moment in *Mother Courage* when Swiss Cheese is taken loses its emotional impact if the actor playing him shows any foreboding when he speaks to his sister Kattrin in Scene Three (pp. 32–3). 'It seems hard for an actor to repress his pity for the character he is playing and not to reveal his knowledge of his impending death,' wrote Brecht.[141]

> 'What can destroy an audience's independence is the actor or director's sentimentalism.'[142]
>
> Declan Donnellan

Reading the play out loud in a group makes it seem more alive on the page, and regular reading is an ongoing activity to do both privately and collectively, each time revealing something new, as things previously unnoticed emerge and strike a different chord or create fresh layers of understanding, prompting ideas and choices. Keep in mind the story and the function and force of each character as you read. In rehearsals, make time to tell the story of individual characters. In telling the story of a character you send their story through your system and begin to own it.

Decanting characters

> '*I want [actors] to take care of the play, not the character. I want them to tell a story.*'[143]
>
> Patrick Marber

Getting familiar with the text outside of rehearsals is like conducting an investigation, combing the text for clues and bringing discoveries and questions back into the developing rehearsal process. Documenting what the play says about a character is standard procedure for actors cast in a particular role and a task that directors undertake for all the characters. This is factual information gathered from the text, not born from any supposition or conjecture. Players' imaginations should be harnessed to work in the rehearsal room rather than fabricating additional material which is not in the play. You are not constructing a complete biography since you have only snippets of information. It is a forensic examination identifying what is made available on the pages of the script, finding out what characters do or what the dramatist tells us about them, either directly or through other characters. Sometimes the smallest of details reveal the essence of a character. Edward Bond's stage directions are precise. When, in *Saved*, Len joins Fred fishing at the lake in the park at the beginning of Scene Six, the directions for Fred read: '*he takes a cigarette from the pack in his pocket without taking the packet out*' (p. 63). Clearly he is well practised in having a cigarette without offering the packet to anyone else. His whole attitude to life is expressed concretely in this one action.

> '*You can only find out what's in a play from the words of the play.*'[144]
>
> Mike Alfreds

Motivation is often not clear-cut. Playwrights often don't know why characters do certain things. Characters may have multi-intentions in a moment and are not necessarily aware of their own needs. Players need to lose themselves in the action and allow the character to emerge and develop through that process. The story needs to go forwards not backwards. What the characters hope for as the outcome of their actions is often a better guide than trying to piece together the events of their fictional past.

However, the concept of a 'backstory' can be valuable when information in the play actually refers to the past, such as when Mother

Courage mentions that Kattrin is 'only dumb from war, soldier stuffed something in her mouth when she was little' (p.59), or for characters in a relationship with a shared history, such as Gertrude and Claudius in *Hamlet*, or Harry and Mary in *Saved*. So hunting down clues during reading is necessary. Be careful only to look for things justified by the text: use only the facts that are mentioned in the script. The lure of backstory is a cul-de-sac unless anchored to concrete moments in the play itself. Beckett wrote cuttingly of an interview with Sir Ralph Richardson in which the famous actor asked about the biography of Pozzo, and Beckett responded that all he knew was in the text and if he had known any more that's where he would have put it. What is in the text are references to the fact that both couples in *Waiting for Godot* have a history of long association in a shared past. For instance, Vladimir once threw himself into the River Rhone and Estragon fished him out, perhaps illustrating that contemplating suicide has been an option in the past. They refer to harvesting grapes together and climbing the Eiffel Tower, while Lucky has been Pozzo's 'sidekick' for over fifty years. These are the facts as given in the text.

The important thing is what you do with the information. When directing, Simon Callow asks actors to write the story of the play through their charac-ter's viewpoint, in essence constructing a path through the play and their relationships to other characters. Other directors ask actors to tell the story of their character to the ensemble. This idea is adapted in the following exercise, tracking the journey of characters through what happens in the story without writing it out in prose. It can be done outside of rehearsals with the results brought in to be shared and compared.

> '*If the information is not given in the playtext, it can't be important.*'[145]
>
> William H. Macy

Character tracking

Players are given A4 paper and turn it in landscape mode. They fold the paper in half.

On the left-hand side, players bullet-point the significant events that an audience would see occurring in each scene. Avoid lengthy descriptions and focus on key moments. It is important to note only what an audience sees happening visually, not what the character is thinking or feeling but what they do.

The right-hand side is where players jot down any related events or incidents undertaken by other characters that impact on what their own character does.

Although in some cases this exercise can take considerable time, even tackling it for an individual scene has benefits in encouraging players to focus on what they need to communicate to the audience visually. Individual work like this is essential, and every actor is familiar with having to do their 'homework'. Whatever method you use for documenting characters, utilising what is gleaned for the whole company and pooling ideas will offer insights relevant for the whole play. Imagery associated with specific characters is a fertile source for exploratory work, for example. The principle of sharing information and working on it collectively is invaluable, and tends to happen verbally during the course of rehearsals as players bring their findings to what they do. More concrete ways are helpful as reminders: lists and stuff pinned up on the rehearsal room wall, added to visual books or mood boards, shared via web forums, or presented as illustrated storyboards, are all grist to the mill. Education packs to support company productions often raid these, adding rehearsal notes and interviews to provide resources for their target audiences.

Once cast, individual players take on charting the physical and emotional journey of a character, or characters, they will play. This is where you begin probing characters from a variety of different angles and experiment, what Eugenio Barba calls the 'composition process'. Barba asserts that the great actors of the Western tradition 'did not and do not begin with the interpretation of the character, but develop their work following a route... based on... assembling aspects that would at first seem incoherent from the point of view of habitual realism, and ending with a formally coherent synthesis.'[146] Discoveries mean little until players are able to sort out how they affect them physically – actors need to begin to feel like someone else.

Characters in motion

'The really exciting response always comes from physicalising something: that's when something hits visually.'[147]

Simon Russell Beale

However astute players may be at discussing characters and however enjoyable they find exercises like 'hot-seating', their physical posture and gait as well as their voice frequently stay remarkably like themselves. Three major pitfalls arise with work on physical character: cliché, personal habits and playing safe. Exercises such as 'walking like the character' are far too general to be of real value and often result in clichéd stereotypes. Playing around to find what part of the body a character might lead with, as in the upcoming exercise, is more fruitful and has the effect of altering the stance and way of walking. It is common to find players make similar physical choices for different characters, so they need a critical awareness of their own predilections and habits so as to avoid relying on these rather than searching out more daring options. What characters require is not necessarily obvious. For example, a high-status character is not always best served by pulling up and becoming 'taller'; this might be more suited to someone with aspirations. No one gets it right first time. Discoveries aren't instantaneous. Being bold requires an ability to take risks and not worry about the result, and failures are often where you make the deepest discoveries. Brave choices come from directing creative energy and playfulness into the process, as in the exercises that follow.

'It's okay to fail – that's how we can make more daring choices.'[148]

Sam Mendes

There are a huge number of approaches to finding a physical orientation for a character. Animal parallels, an object lying around the rehearsal room, a pair of someone else's shoes, a photograph, a line of text are all valid starting points. One player may be inspired by a momentary feeling caught in the midst of a game or improvising a situation in the play; another may discover the physical essence of a character through the way their breathing changes. Decanting characters provides the evidence which may prompt ideas. Those ideas need to be translated into sensations. Sensations are felt in the body. Investigating where a character's weight is concentrated and how that alters their centre of gravity, or discovering a dominant energy, can all provoke sensations and energies. For example, Vladimir is more upright and orientated skywards whereas Estragon, despite being lighter than Vladimir (who says 'You're lighter than I am' as they consider hanging for the first time (p. 17)), is more ponderous and focused towards the earth. Marlene's statement to Isabella Bird on the first page of *Top Girls* that 'I can't bear sitting still' (p. 1) gives a clear indication of her inner energy. Experimenting with alternative possibilities in displacing your habitual muscular disposition means you can move towards transforming yourself. Linda Marlowe talks of finding an 'exaggerated repetitive gesture... that doesn't end up in the production but is a way of orientating myself'.[149]

Physicality of characters evolves during rehearsals and is gradually modified and developed; the work is ongoing and, rather than something you can simply front-load, needs to be integral to the process and allied to imaginative use of the text. This is where working through playful improvisations to connect the body and the imagination pays dividends. It is the physical imagination of players which needs to be set free.

Once players are cast, the following exercise is a good starting point. Used as a preliminary exercise in establishing characters' physicality, it gives players something to work with. Returning to it as rehearsals progress and inviting players to reconsider their initial choices is extremely important. As they continue working on the play, they discover more about the characters and revising decisions is part of the process.

Body-part leading

Line up players on one side of the room.

Everyone walks across the room to the opposite side and back again by leading with their nose.

Discuss how this makes them feel and what kind of character it represents.

Then repeat the walk but this time leading with the chin. And then try leading with the elbow. Then the pelvis. Then the knees. Then the toes. And finally the bum.

This last one is quite difficult and doesn't simply mean walking backwards with the bum sticking out. But discovering how to travel with the bum leading makes players aware of turning the head to see, and can create a sense of someone anxious, even paranoid.

Now players think about which point of the body the character might lead with, and practise the walk across the room accordingly.

Another popular way in which characters' physicality can be accessed is in exercises where animal parallels are employed, a practice used in drama schools and by many practitioners. Lecoq begins with the animal's 'purchase on the ground', its stance, connection with the earth, shape of foot, and then draws analogies with humans: hooves which trot are suggestive of women in heels, a duck's web-footed gait is reminiscent of Charlie Chaplin's gait.[150]

Taking animal characteristics into the body by adjusting posture affects the way you breathe, stand, walk, do anything; imagining an animal's 'pulse rate' as the tempo for movement encourages players to break their personal and

> *'The physical variations in the animal kingdom are extremely marked and therefore easy to latch on to.'*[151]
>
> Harriet Walter

habitual physical mould. Finding different movements associated with an animal, such as tilting the head sideways (dog), or leading with the nose (fox), alters the inner dynamic meaning that such 'tiny physical adjustments can take you inside a character'.[152] Attention to detail in imitation from observation is important; while there is no need for an audience to identify the animal chosen by a player, if the detail is right something may strike a chord with them and they will recognise 'someone like that'. However, as Jean Newlove points out 'slavish copying... is not enough to convey meaning,' and advises actors to 'probe beyond the outer shell and search for an inner attitude... directly linked to the movement observed.'[153] So while playing animals is fun in a workshop, transposing the dynamic of the animal's physicality to a human character can be tricky; the following exercise is designed to assist that process.

Animal on a lead

If you haven't yet cast the play, draw character names from a hat and distribute. Alternatively, work on one character at a time and compare the choices made by individuals.

Step 1

Each player chooses an animal they decide represents the character they are working on or have been allocated. Players need time to visit the zoo or at least access video footage of their chosen animal to observe and take notes about how the animal stands, poses, moves and reacts if possible.

Step 2

Once in rehearsal, players imagine their animal tied to a lead around 1–1.5 metres long. As they hold their end of the lead, players follow the imaginary animal as it explores the space and anything in it.

As the animal moves about – sits, lies, runs, leaps, wallows, flies – players are forced to experiment with differing postures and rhythms to accommodate its journey around the room and its antics.

Once players appear to be capturing some of the energy of their animal, invite players to start to explore the difference between letting the animal pull them in different directions and points where they might pull the animal away from things or bring them 'to heel'.

This exercise is not about imitating an animal but about finding an inner dynamic in terms of rhythm and pace, which feels like a new 'skin'. Once players have discovered a physicality to embody this, they can dispense with the imaginary lead yet maintain the sense of the inner dynamic they experienced to explore movement in space. It's important here to recapture the play of tensions between being pulled across the space in different directions or being pulled up short by the imaginary animal suddenly stopping, or pulling on the lead to restrain the animal, as this relates to how characters might feel they are in control, or feel they are being controlled, or even that unnerving feeling of veering out of control.

Discoveries made can be enhanced by playing a game with everyone in their newly found character's 'skin'. Grandmother's Footsteps works well at this point since it's a game demanding control and economy in moving as well as finding the balance of standing still in a new stance.

'There should be no distinction drawn between the ways that an actor might understand character by way of textual analysis and physical analysis and experimentation.'[154]

Scott Graham and Steve Hoggett

Sensations in the body are central to accessing what we might call physical truth. Playing with the fullest physical spectrum offers a wealth of perspectives on stylistic choices, and working with different scales is a powerful rehearsal tool. The animal-inspired characters can be imported to the next exercise in order to explore this.

Percentage play

Players maintain the physical characteristics they have found via their animal-on-a-lead as a basis for this exercise.

Players imagine this character alone. Find a simple everyday activity to do in that place that is not related to anything in the text, the simpler the better. The activity should not be something relating to the period of the play or any objects or activities in the play; so, for example, Lady Macbeth should not have a letter but she might be ironing. The action should be one that can be easily mimed. If players feel they need an object then use something in the room to represent the item – such as a shoe for the iron.

Relax in the place and discover a way of repeating the activity in a repeatable cycle. At this stage it is as though the character is almost resting in the activity so that it seems very natural and doesn't require very much energy.

This is thirty per cent on a scale of one to one hundred per cent.

Now vary the intensity of the physical activity using the full scale of the range. Taking it down to one per cent will produce real subtlety, expanding to two hundred per cent should produce something quite monstrous. Try not to fall in the trap of speeding up the activity. This is not about pace but intensity.

Here the search is for the physical truth of a simple activity, such as ironing. You can apply it later on to use something featured in a play, such as washing hands in the case of Lady Macbeth. The reason for not starting with an activity actually in the play is to establish the principle without investing emotion (which actors will be tempted to do if you allow them); that comes later.

The concept of scale is enormously useful when trying to move away from literal responses. Percentages can be applied at various points when experimenting with levels of intensity to tone down or increase energy or to find extremes in physicality. On the surface, *The Importance of Being Earnest* might appear a straightforward comedy of manners, yet the Kaos Theatre production's sophisticated level of grotesque satire is illustrated by the moment when Lady Bracknell pronounced the famous line 'A handbag!' hoisted like a huge puppet over the heads of other players. This company regularly played with percentages during rehearsals. Actor and teacher Jane Hartley suggests starting at fifty per cent and working up to one hundred or even two hundred per cent, and scaling right down to one per cent to find a maximum degree of subtlety. As she points out: 'there might be a time during the performance where it's appropriate that you take something up to one hundred per cent, another where you need only five per cent'.[155] Using a wide range of percentages rather than the numerical scale of one to ten enables players to find extremes through exaggeration so they discover the necessity of precision and clarity, the need to use their body with discipline and economy.

Things out of scale on stage are visually intriguing. Robert Wilson's production of *Woyzeck* opened with the Fairground Barker on stilts, a distortion to establish a surreal world in which Woyzeck was fed peas by a double-headed Doctor played by two actors literally stuck together like Siamese twins encased in one specially tailored costume. At times a puppet doppelgänger for Tom Waits appeared singing the music. The concept of scale becomes invaluable in the next section on workshopping scenes as a way to explore visually dynamic staging.

Characters in context

Characters don't operate in a vacuum, but emerge through interaction. They are interconnected: not only do they function in relation to the story but in relation to each other, and it is often in the contrasts between characters that their individuality surfaces. They are revealed via their relationships with each other, by the energy they transmit and the force they represent which relates to the central core of the play. Finding their individual 'force field' comes through interaction and relationships with others on stage.

> *'Action in drama is usually interpersonal; one character does or says something to another.'*[156]
>
> Sam Smiley

The deference of those around a ruler conveys the ruler's superiority. In the currency of familial and social relationships, shifts in control or power have more subtlety, and status is less obvious but nonetheless evident. Keith Johnstone's analysis of status as a behavioural transaction and his suggestions for improvisatory work to establish experiential understanding of how status operates is illuminating; I refer anyone unfamiliar with his book *Impro* to the opening chapter, since a strong grasp of status is invaluable. To illustrate the see-saw nature of transactions in a text, Johnstone uses exchanges between Vladimir and Estragon in the first few pages of *Waiting for Godot* where they bicker like a married couple about who hurts the most. Throughout the play they banter and play games with the familiarity of old friends. Yet although superficially they appear as a double act, they are not merely two sides of the same coin. They are counterpointed physically by their differing energies and moves.

The play is an intensely animated one given that it's famously one in which nothing appears to happen. Various accounts of Beckett directing this play report he had actors on their feet, experimenting with movement and rhythms, working like a choreographer in measuring steps taken and playing with gesture; there was no sitting round a table analysing the meaning or probing the thoughts and feelings of characters, and rehearsals were active searches for what he called 'themes of the body'. The lyricism of the play lies as much in its visual as its linguistic musicality, and Beckett makes constant use of the language of physical imagery. Charting the physicality of his two central characters reveals how visual imagery structures their journey, the visual motifs and geometric patterns of movement that echo from one moment to another. Vladimir and Estragon are effectively 'caged', their movements circumscribed. Vladimir moves in curvilinear lines and never sits on the stone alone, whereas Estragon moves in straight lines, frequently sitting alone on the stone. While Estragon may be less physically energetic, he is temperamentally more volatile and Vladimir more assertive. It is Vladimir who first suggests hanging.

To 'choreograph the knowledge' relates to communicating key narrative events or factual information in charting journeys. Beckett's concept of 'themes of the body' suggests a way of charting physical motifs that can augment the visual iconography. This is applied in more detail in later sections, which feature the potential for conveying physical manifestations of characteristics, interrelationships and shifts in character, as well as ideas for reinforcing the dominant thematic concerns and for moving stories forward visually.

'It is through relationships that one develops character.'[157]

Harriet Walter

Players receive impressions and respond to various stimuli, and, crucially, to each other: as Harriet Walter says, 'the most important work happens in the rehearsal room, through interaction... I may well find the key to my character in another actor's eyes, in the way he or she looks at me'.[158] Every change in one character provokes a reaction in another character. A reaction may not be articulated yet it is thought, and thought is grounded in the body. The impact of gesture is not simply found in the expression of an individual player but in the muscular dialogue generated through interaction between players. Characters exhibit thought in actions, whether at the level of the tiniest movement or a leap onto the table; an exchange between players via a look or glance can be as powerful as a jump and catch. The action of thinking might be impetuous or deliberate, depending on the context in which the decision is being made and on the personal traits and attributes imbued in the character. The way the action of thinking is played is a stylistic feature, but what leads the player are sensations felt through the body as it is engaged in action. Muscles think.

Characters are conceived in relation to one another and the world/society around them. How each character relates to others is the key: it indicates how they will stand in relation

> 'Thought in a character begins as sentience, or sensory perception.'[159]
>
> Sam Smiley

to each other on stage and their disposition towards each other. Characters need to be developed alongside each other, as Brecht reminds us: 'For the smallest social unit is not the single person but two people. In life we develop one another.'[160]

Partnerships between two characters in some kind of relationship, familial/marital/professional and so on, feature in most plays. Couples are caught up in various situations at different points in a play. Improvising situations between two characters promotes active experimentation; connections to plot and attitudes to themes are embedded in their interactions. More work on character interactions in scenes comes up in sections that follow. At this point keep the focus on key moments in the tapestry of the whole. A similar exercise to the *Flash-plays* and *Ten-point trailers* in Section 3 comes next. Here players search out significant points from the perspective of a pair of characters. If attention has focused predominantly on central protagonists and those closest to them in rehearsals so far, choosing duos from other partnerships for this exercise opens up the play, teasing out contrasts and allusions hitherto neglected and illuminating the theme with new concerns. Examples from the plays under discussion might be Harry and Mary in *Saved*, Marie and the Drum Major in *Woyzeck*, Marco and Rodolpho in *A View from the Bridge*, Hamlet and Horatio or Laertes and Ophelia in *Hamlet*.

Navigation plays

Players work in pairs on two characters who share a relationship in the play.

Using the text as a springboard, work out the point where the relationship is established for the audience and moments where there are significant action points in terms of an identifiable shift or change in the relationship as the play progresses and/or points where its stability is reinforced or broken. If there are points at which one character leaves or someone dies (such as Laertes leaving Paris and later returning to find Ophelia dead), don't stop at that point – find a way of showing the remaining character when there is a point that illustrates their loss.

Create a sequence of physical movements, without speaking the text, to demonstrate these moments. These can be highly energetic leaps and catches if you are working in that mode or strings of less energetic movements involving various forms of contact, looks and gestures. You may end up pacing round each other like panthers or glaring across space in quiet stillness, or using a slight movement, such as brushing your partner's shoulder.

These physical sequences without words highlight the relationship through choreographed movement. Use the strategy of finding a moment of stillness to indicate a break between moments as in the flash-plays.

As with previous work on the environment, search for the essence of things in imaginative ways rather than trying to 'stage' scenes between characters. Try to ensure players are exploiting the stage dynamics established in earlier work on space. This does not necessarily mean throwing each other around but creating spatially dynamic interactions.

A point worth noting is that eye contact, or lack of it, is a significant indicator of levels of intimacy. As Alan Ayckbourn observes, 'Very few of us maintain eye contact for very long. If we do, it should mean something dramatically: we are in love, we fear attack, we don't understand what they're telling us, we can't believe our eyes.'[161] Imagining the whole body like a six-foot face or applying percentages to the way you use eye contact forces communication through deliberate movements.

This is to be encouraged, though it is always important to apply economy in terms of the precision with which moves are executed; that way you convey things with clarity. Expansive and exaggerated gestures are not to be discouraged as long as they avoid cliché – toning down expression is much easier than trying to increase it later on.

Characters and feelings

'Feelings, states and passions are expressed through gestures, attitudes and movements similar to those of physical actions.'[162]

Jacques Lecoq

Approaching feeling directly by attempting to manufacture emotions is a blind alley: as Declan Donnellan memorably puts it, 'It is no more possible to express emotion than it is to shit through your ear.'[163] You can't play feelings, only actions. Beware of trying to 'identify' with the emotional aspects. If the moment is poignant, it is because the playwright has set it up as such, so pretending to be upset simply tells the audience twice and they switch off. The precise arrangement of circumstances constructed by the playwright in the immediate actions of the play stimulates feelings as a by-product. Feelings surface in the body through playing actions – in other words, what a character *does* in that situation. Enacting a situation jogs various muscles, and feelings and emotions are associated with and linked to muscular configurations in the body. Obvious examples are laughing and crying, which are both activated by muscles around the diaphragm. As work progresses, players experience effects that will lead to the discovery of moments where passions rise up unbidden. Monitoring these is an ongoing process. The patterns of emotional journeys are woven from a combination of visual and physical images and verbal utterance. Charting emotional journeys for characters means finding what might move, disturb, or even wound the spectator in physical gestural language. This may be as minimal as a sharp intake of breath. The example from John Wright where students actors found the 'game of breathing' mentioned in Section 2 is pertinent here.

'The situation tells us what you're feeling better than you can.'[164]

John Wright

This is not to say actors should never invoke their own experience in imagining an emotional state of a character. We've all wept or raged at various points in our lives and observed others doing so, so we all have a bank of sensory experiences to draw upon. Most importantly this should not be the only resource. An actor's experience stops short of where a character's emotional journey might lead. Observation is key: Helene Weigel was inspired by a newspaper photograph of an Indian woman keening over the body of her son killed during the shelling of Singapore in creating the famous 'silent scream' when Mother Courage hears the shots which kill her son Swiss Cheese.

The points at which characters make a decision significant to the plot are key moments when feelings and thoughts coalesce in action. Sam Smiley, the playwright and screenwriter who worked on the early James Bond movies, divides decisions into two categories: expedient and ethical, a useful distinction. Expedient decisions are more often to do with narrative, while ethical decisions are more often related to theme. When characters make choices, their decisions are bound up with rejecting alternatives. Playing actions and exploring situations through physical engagement both generate numerous options; as rehearsals progress players explore these, searching out what lies behind the words to inform the discovery of the impulses that govern the thought patterns of characters, the decisions they make and the words they utter. Intensive work on actions in dialogue and speech follows in Section 6: Inside the Words.

> 'Decision is a moment of focus in which thought and character become action; they initiate change.' [165]
>
> Sam Smiley

Once players have traced a character's journey they will have expanded their knowledge of the play, making connections between how characters serve the narrative, how they travel through it, and how they have changed, or not, by the end of the play. Along the way, discoveries about how characters relate to one another, moments where characters undergo significant changes, and experience key turning points, and reactions to these will all surface. As physical characteristics begin to evolve, initial choices will inevitably mutate and alter as more layers of text are uncovered, but provide something to work on. Putting all this into practice in a virtual run of the play is worth the effort. Use a similar framework to the *Route map* from the mapping section to sketch the progress of characters through entrances and exits on an empty stage. By now players have begun absorbing characters so this is an opportunity to test out some of their inklings and ideas as they feel their way through the play. Run this when there is plenty of time and ensure everyone is very focused.

Greetings

Using the concept of the *Route map* from Section 3, gather the cast around a horseshoe-shaped stage area. Use a Caller as you did in that exercise to announce the act, scene and cue line when every character comes on and goes off.

At each entrance and with each exit characters embody reactions to each other non-verbally, based on their knowledge of the character to date and embodying what their expectations are at this point in the play. While they skip the meat of the scene they still play the reactions to each other and to the arrival or departure of each character, so the instruction to allow a 'beat' to register the impact of each entrance and exit is important.

This is an opportunity for players to string together the key points in a character's journey and see how different facets surface. By all means put on music at a low level in the background – some players find this helps their concentration and removes any self-consciousness they may feel – but make sure it is something instrumental with a fairly innocuous beat.

Players interact with more purpose than in *Route map* and are beginning to 'fill the form' of the outline structure. Points where moods are established and broken, or seem to fall over each other, emerge in the rhythm of comings and goings; everyone gains a sense of undercurrents in the flow of the play as this starts becoming apparent. The way characters greet each other reveals burgeoning relationships – particularly for any pairings who have worked on the exercise *Navigation plays* – as their stories emerge through visual reactions. Individual players begin to sense the idea of moving through peaks and troughs, noting landmark moments where characters encounter a change of fortune, change of allegiance, change of heart, change of mind; moments where something threatens to pull them back from actions, moments where irresistible forces compel them towards certain actions. Sensations experienced during this exercise further players' acquaintance with characters from the perspective of taking them *inside* the play.

Rerunning this play-without-words at key stages in a rehearsal process gives opportunities to test out ideas in actions and gestures, to experiment with deeper connections players are making to the whole play as the characters grow. Each replaying reveals new and richer layers. The inherent dynamic in every entrance and exit develops as these become part of the structure of a performance continuum, active agents in modifying pace and tempo, causing shifts in the rhythm of a play.

'Action is the principle definer of character in a play.'[167]

Steve Gooch

As established in the previous section, dialogue is the top line of the score; beneath it lie a whole unwritten score of actions. In an interview with Richard Eyre about acting, Dame Judi Dench uses the analogy of, 'that cake called *mille feuille*, which is made of many layers of thin pastry', and says, 'you don't play what's on the page... it's as if the line is the bit of icing on the top'.[166] The work undertaken in charting the journeys augments knowledge gained through mapping the play by identifying characters' actions in broad strokes, creating those underlying layers. In a performance there will be moments where an audience know, without a character saying anything, what is going on inside them. In searching out the trajectory of characters in a play you begin to find how to transmit their thoughts and passions through what they do.

The focus in the next section shifts to working on scenes to discover a play's potential style and interpretation before tackling what lies inside and around the words.

Section 5

Workshopping Scenes

Workshopping Scenes

This section relies on an acquaintance with mapping and charting, and explores the impact of bodies on stage in more detail. Players should arrive at working on scenes with a strong idea of the general flow of the play's narrative and relationships. The raw material created through previous work will no doubt prompt ideas for opening up the territory of individual scenes and can be raided or discarded as rehearsals develop and players move closer to speaking the words on the page.

Work here is orientated to exploring actions and imagery with some approaches to visual composition. These ideas and suggestions are not designed as foolproof rehearsal strategies; some are more suited to some plays than others, and some may challenge received ideas or perceptions about particular plays or styles of performance. The aim is to activate players' creative and thinking muscles on the basic premise that the most surprising discoveries about a play, or ways to play a play, are often revealed by indirect approaches. Underlying the work is the principle of being open to possibilities.

'We knew our way round the scripts in terms of geographical coordinates. We knew the terrain.'[168]

Declan Donnellan

'Plays have actions but so do scenes.'[169]

David Edgar

Each scene works like a mini-play, telling an episode or fragment of the story, but without completion since what happens in one scene provokes what happens in another, or begs questions later scenes might answer. The task is to uncover what new knowledge or circumstances appear to upset any balance already established together with the sequence of changes and transformations that jostle one another in an individual scene or segue into the next.

Each scene/episode can be mapped and character journeys charted in a similar manner to that work on the whole play. A scene is purposefully constructed, posing questions to be developed or answered at a later point. Players should be careful about dragging knowledge of what comes later into an earlier scene – therein lies the potential danger of giving the game away to an audience. Any prefiguring or foregrounding will become apparent in performance as the play unfolds for them in time without the need to underline it. Considering each scene in isolation and each with its own particular task best serves the play: as David Mamet says, 'After you finish a scene, you will encounter another one with its *own* task; the total of these is the play. If you play each scene [in isolation from the others], the play will be served.'[170]

Scene stories

There is no particular virtue in starting at the beginning and working consecutively through scenes in a play (opening scenes are given attention in Section 8:

'Each scene in a play, like each cell in a body, is an embodiment of that play as a whole.'[171]

Steve Waters

Shaping and Pacing). One scene may stand out as capturing the essence of the play so that is often a good place to start; alternatively, dive in and tackle the most challenging one. If you need to divide up a play without scene demarcations, length is immaterial; what is important is the need for a scene or unit to encompass some kind of change, i.e. a coherent segment embodying at least one moment of change. Superficially it may seem nothing much changes in a play like *Waiting for Godot*, and this is where thinking about the audience is crucial: as the action inches forward they accumulate more and more questions, processing incremental differences as well as any repetitions. This requires separating segments of the script by assessing how these variances operate, ascertaining where the balance and equilibrium of the whole play is tested in the concerns of individual sections. Beckett divided up Act One into six 'scenes' and Act Two into five when he directed the play himself, each a rhythmic unit.

Wherever you begin, start with a bare stage; if the play requires specific set items, such as the cart in *Mother Courage* or the tree and stone in *Waiting for Godot* or the bed in *Blasted*, the humble chair or stage blocks are perfectly adequate stand-ins. Resist the temptation to 'end-gain' by starting to work through a scene with the dialogue and attempting to stage it. This leads to simply joining up the dots. A richer end product comes from viewing a scene from every possible angle – you see more each time – before beginning to make decisions that will fix it.

'*The way I work now is non-prescriptive and non-linear.*'[172]

Sam Mendes

Clarity is born from a really secure grasp of the segment of story that is told by an individual scene. Playful ways of telling and retelling stories pave the way for embedding that clarity – the following game works well in a warm-up preceding work on a scene and players may be familiar with it if they have played the Keepy-uppy game described after *Ten-point trailers* in Section 3 (p. 57). This time it comes in two versions: once the first is mastered, the second one can be used for retelling in subsequent rehearsals, or you can make up similar ones with a beanbag or ball.

Balloon stories

The game is to keep the balloon off the ground while telling the story of the scene in the same way as in the ball game called Keepy-uppy, except that a balloon is more difficult to control than a ball. Divide up into groups of four or five – the groups who complete the storytelling with the least number of restarts wins.

Version 1: Players use only their hands to keep the balloon airborne, and tell the story as they do this, with all players taking responsibility for keeping the story going, whether or not they are actually touching the balloon. The idea is to keep the story going and the balloon in the air with as much momentum as possible. If the balloon hits the floor, restart the scene story from the beginning again. An additional rule of calling a 'fault' if the story reaches a hiatus of more than five seconds can be applied; this requires everyone to have a sure grasp of what happens in the scene.

Version 2: Players use any part of the body *except the hands* (e.g. feet, knees, elbows, bums) to keep the balloon airborne, and tell the story as they do this. As in the previous version, when the balloon hits the floor, restart the scene story from the beginning again.

Each time the scene is retold in this way, expect and relish any differences. When bits of the story are left out it usually signals players are unsure about a particular section, and work can be directed towards sorting out the problem. As players gain more confidence and familiarity with the chain of events in a scene, they become much more concerned with keeping the balloon off the ground and achieving the goal of the game and the story starts to flow underneath.

The word commonly used for fixing stage movement in the initial phase of putting scenes on their feet is 'blocking'. The theatrical meaning derives from a nineteenth-century practice of designating all stage move-

'Blocking has unfortunate connotations of blocked paths and blocked creative juices.'[173]

Harriet Walter

ment with blocks of wood to represent the actors prior to rehearsals. As Mike Alfreds notes, 'It blocks possibilities of creative change, of spontaneity, of life itself.'[174]

Layering is a more productive term for experimenting at this stage to allow staging arrangements to emerge organically. Players need to explore the substance of scenes simultaneously with developing movement and character interactions; by this process they will make discoveries through finding gestures, working with each other, with objects, and with words, all within the framework of storytelling. The process of rehearsing is to investigate and explore, repeat and examine, investigate some more, revise and repeat, examine and repeat, repeat and revise, revise and repeat, etc. Getting it wrong is inherent to the creative process, and as John Berger points out, 'Inspiration is the capacity to recognise the mistakes.'[175]

'You have to be open enough and confident enough not to pin things down too early.'[176]

Cath Binks

Players thrive on approaches which fire imaginative and sensory responses. One of Lepage's standard techniques in rehearsals is an exercise where actors sketch out images of the source material/text using marker pens. A few marker pens and end-rolls of wallpaper or sketchpads are welcome additions in a rehearsal room; you will find that large-sized paper garners more physical engagement with the tasks and usually produces more expressive results.

A diagrammatic graph of a scene equips everyone with a tangible sense of its overall shape with its peaks, troughs and flatlines. The next exercise prepares the ground for undertaking this. You need three varied instrumental tracks of around two to three minutes each for this, preferably pieces unfamiliar to the group and with variance in their beats per minute (BPM). One from the classical repertoire, one from jazz and one from electronic dance is a workable combination;[177] tracks from film scores work equally well providing players don't know them (otherwise they can't help recalling the film!) – so choose less obvious ones.

Musical graphs

Players lie relaxed on the floor, eyes closed. Each has three sheets of paper (not smaller than A4) and a marker pen beside them (marker pens with thick nibs are best). Ensure everyone understands the purpose is not about whether the tracks appeal to them or not in terms of their musical tastes, but about listening to the inherent dynamic – how the music unfolds in time.

Play the three tracks, pausing after each one for a couple of minutes. In those couple of minutes in between tracks, players take the marker pen 'for a walk' across the paper drawing a graphic representation to capture the variances in intensity of the one they have just heard. Use the paper in landscape mode and travel the marker pen from left to right. This should be done swiftly.

Wait until the last is completed before discussing the results.

As you compare and discuss responses, individual tastes will probably crop up. It's really important to get past this: it is not about likes and dislikes, but how each track unfolds. Similarities between the diagrams for the same tracks become apparent even though drawing styles vary. Through examining the differences between three tracks, players pick up on the varied nature of dynamic structures, and the effects of diverse rhythmic patterns. This is indispensable when shaping and pacing individual scenes and eventually the whole play.

'The dynamic structures in music arrangements are a precious tool for us.'[178]

Scott Graham and Steven Hoggett

Scene graphs

Follow up the musical graphs with players drawing a visual graph of the scene you are working on – after reading it through but before you attempt to run it, with the same instruction to draw on a blank sheet of paper from left to right. The left-to-right instruction echoes the movement through time.

It doesn't matter how crude these are: some people produce neatly organised maps and others are more messy.

As with musical graphs, the benefit lies in engaging with an exercise that transforms the scene into another medium. Any sharing and discussion of variances in diagrams and the responses of players to the task is invaluable. The points at which shifts and different directions in the lines on the graphs occur is important for later work in the next section, as well as what happens in this one.

'We concentrate on the events and tasks [which] are the deeper structures that run beneath the surface of the words.'[179]

Katie Mitchell

The next two exercises develop active engagement with the patterns of peaks and troughs in these drawings. For the purposes of exploring the underbelly of text you don't need to be musicians – imaginative use of everyday objects can create a junk orchestra: flapping the pages of a newspaper, banging a pen or pencil on a hard surface, drumming fingers, slapping thighs all have percussive qualities that can be harnessed for the following exercises. These are modified versions of exercises published in *Through the Body*.[180] As stated there, Scenes One, Four and Five from Act One of *Hamlet* work very well for this, but the work is suited not only to these or 'meaty' scenes which contain key events, like the banquet scene in *Macbeth*; in less dramatically conventional plays such as *Waiting for Godot* this exercise reveals interesting undulations. Use the same scene from the previous exercise for these scene-scapes, or divide up sizeable coherent sections of it to distribute between several groups if the scene is very long.

Junk orchestral scene-scape

Distribute a selection of percussion tools and /or instruments – home-made ones are as effective as the orchestral varieties – anything that can be shaken, rattled, banged or chimed will do, but ensure you have a variety of sounds. Players can also use their bodies, drum on the floor or on furniture, etc.

Each group reads through the scene – out loud is best – before pin-pointing major moments of tension (which will be evident in the peaks of their graphic outline) and identifying any portion that seems to 'flat-line', noting points where something changes or shifts. As with the *Flash-plays* in Section 3, a time limit helps to focus the work – this will depend on the length of the scene chosen, but around fifteen minutes should be enough.

Once these are agreed, the group attempts to label each section using a single active verb. For example, Act One, Scene Four of *Hamlet* might end up in six segments labelled: Waiting, Debating, Seeing, Beckon-ing, Fighting, Following. This is crucial – it's not giving the segments titles (as in the Kaos example mentioned earlier, e.g. 'the muffins scene'), because here you are concerned with what is happening.

Having established and labelled the segments, groups use the per-cussion to improvise a soundscape. They will go through a few 'drafts' to create a final piece. Try to avoid the literal, such as replicating the sound of footsteps. Be careful always to be concerned with capturing the ebb and flow of the scene rather than mimicry – it's a soundscape not a sound-picture. A point to bear in mind is whether to punctuate the points between segments with a stop or whether to attempt a smooth transition.

Allow about ten to fifteen minutes for this part of the exercise.

Groups play their compositions to other groups. It is common to find players inflecting the same scene slightly differently although the overall shape is usually similar. A common reaction is to make sound-scapes overly busy as people tend to fight shy of using silence; when they do have the courage to incorporate silence, the results are invariably more powerful – and discovering that 'less is more' is a valuable lesson. Silence is rather like stillness in theatre: two dimensions which relate to building tension and suspense. The decision about punctuating points or effecting smooth transitions is one to note in terms of the effects created.

> '*Follow the rhythm of the story and give expression to the action.*'[181]
>
> Bertolt Brecht

Scene-scape

Here groups search out physical equivalents for the sounds made with junk instruments in terms of the ebb and flow of tensions. In the case of the example from *Hamlet*, these are the labels Waiting, Debating, etc. The aim is to capture the rhythm of the scene in movement rather than merely miming actions. Movement can be quite abstract. Use no words.

Players may represent characters, or decide to work in pairs or as a chorus, or a combination of both. Use percussion to accompany or punctuate the movement.

Allow plenty of time for this work – thirty to forty minutes or even longer depending on the length of the scene.

Devoting time to these exercises pays dividends later. They focus attention on the atmosphere and undercurrents in a scene: the push and pull of tensions operating beneath the surface of spoken words, and those points where one segment fades and another begins. Players gain a tangible sense of ways in which rhythm and counter-rhythm underpin everything, which will impact on how action and counter-action operate in later explorations; improvisation work on scenes becomes more vivid than working simply from a reading, laced with a quality that offers emotional and physical insights.

'Carve up the big tasks into small tasks and perform these small tasks.'[182]

David Mamet

Breaking down a script into units, i.e. a section in which a single event occurs, is a familiar rehearsal technique. Each scene is a series of situations; in breaking it apart into situations and incidents, key plot points start to surface, and these may well tally with those identified during work on the *Flash-plays* and *Ten-point trailers* in mapping work, or with those moments of decision and/or change faced by characters and uncovered during *Charting the journeys*. All these pivotal plot points and decision moments are embedded in the peaks and troughs, turning points or motifs in the play. Superimposing these onto a *Scene graph*, from the earlier exercise (see p. 99), anchors them to the shape of that scene, a visual reminder of where incidents are placed within the rhythm of a scene, and where events change. This serves a similar purpose to a pictorial storyboard, outlining the progression of the action in a scene, but without using illustrations which can pre-empt decisions regarding placement and arrangements. Like all the other visual aids it can be pinned up somewhere.

Scoring action

'Only physical actions, physical truths, and physical belief in them! Nothing more.'[183]

Konstantin Stanislavsky

The purpose of exploring movement non-verbally is to uncover actions underpinning situations and incidents. When companies have a shared movement palette, they can develop a sketch of a scene effectively through whatever training they practise. Theatre Workshop actors were able to mime or dance their way through a scene because of their grounding in Laban technique and ballet. Berkoff trained his London Theatre Group actors in mime and movement for months before mounting his first series of Kafka adaptations and, although he has never had a permanent company, has frequently cast actors who have worked with him previously because they have an understanding of his style. Frantic Assembly conduct exercises (often similar to contact-improvisation techniques) to develop performers in the company's signature physicality so that situations and relationships can be explored through improvisation to create what they call 'movement strings'; these then become raw material from which scenes are eventually choreographed.

'The imposition of silent performance leads the students to discover [a] basic law of theatre; words are born from silence.'[184]

Jacques Lecoq

Improvising the actions, incidents and situations away from the script can be tackled in a number of different ways. Stanislavsky, Meyerhold, Copeau all developed non-verbal improvisations to open up the somatic awareness of their actors, not least when they were searching out ways to convey feeling. Stanislavsky realised that improvisation gave actors quicker and more vital access to the necessary physical awareness and experience of a play's dynamic than round-the-table discussion. As he experimented, analytical discussions were relegated to outside rehearsals, and by the 1930s he had put aside his early techniques, which centred on 'Emotion Memory', or 'Affective Memory', because he found the truthfulness he sought could be better stimulated by the play's immediate action rather than simulated by the actor's personal memories. He invested more trust in the instincts of actors, dispensed with detailed prompt books which dictated minute details of motivations and stage business, and ran rehearsals with a simple outline plan. Transferring the actors' attention away from searching for feelings inside themselves towards fulfilling the demands of the scene in relation to their partners on stage, he found they achieved better and quicker results. Sometimes they played a scene in complete silence using only their eyes; when working on a scene using only key words, the moments between them were filled with meaning and an acute sense of contact and connection between players.

> '*It is possible to have a good grasp of a scene in a totally alien language if the actors' imaginations are genuinely working.*'[185]
>
> Declan Donnellan

Stripping the script down to key words forces players to search out what is happening in a scene without the pressure of speaking the dialogue in full, and results in a very workable skeleton of actions and reactions which become a physical dialogue in space. Use coherent segments of not more than a few pages and tackle each separately for maximum benefits. There are several ways to make use of this next exercise: in this instance the focus is on uncovering actions and reactions, but it can easily be adapted to work on action and subtext, or revisited in relation to theme.

Introduce this exercise by applying it to a scene with a maximum of two characters initially; once players get the hang of how it works they can use it for scenes with more characters. Pairs can work on the same scene and then compare the choices they make in selecting key words for practical analysis; this leads to discoveries of differing interpretations of a scene as well as different ways of revealing the actions and reactions in it.

Stripping the text 1

Players re-read a scene or identifiable unit and identify the ten most significant words in terms of what is happening in the scene. The 'ten-word rule' applies however long the scene or unit, unless you are working with one of half a page or less, in which case three words would suffice. Nouns are most effective for the purposes of this exercise.

The ten words selected now become the script – allocated to characters as they are spoken in the play – and players put the scene into action using just these words. Think about how effectively space can be used between bodies.

This exercise reveals the action of a scene in a series of interactions. The choice of words always provokes interest and discussion. In the majority of cases groups choose single nouns or verbs, and invest them with considerable purpose and intensity with pauses operating in between the actions and reactions that move the scene forward. Occasionally a group will choose a few phrases or even a couple of lines. Finding the action in this way opens up the emotional dimension of a scene as players access the impulses behind action. The active nature of the text comes alive.

There is a follow-up exercise in Section 6: Inside the Words which develops the idea of scoring the action in relation to the emotional undertow in dialogue exchanges between two players. Interplay between players is critical since every character grows – and is in a sense made – in response to other members of the cast.

Framing action

'It is not the words which carry the meaning – it is the actions.'[186]

David Mamet

In scoring actions, stage pictures emerge, and in choreographing knowledge, the composition of bodies and images serves the visual storytelling. Spectators interpret spatial and movement relations between performers, so every individual stance, pose, or interaction needs to be considered from their perspective. The work on space and environments undertaken in Section 3 comes to the fore in developing this. Additionally, questions arise concerning how to move from an epic scale to an intimate or very intense moment within the same scene or even within an individual minute. Playing with the optics of the stage generates visual effects. Whether you are working end-on, traverse or in the round, site those observing the experiments so that they are viewing the stage area from different places and see what the 'frame' offers the spectator from various angles.

In Brecht's notes for *Mother Courage and Her Children*, he writes out the action of every scene in prose, rather like a treatment or synopsis, then explains how individual situations and incidents work for the audience in visual and physical terms, how everything from the position of the cart to the mannerisms of characters is arranged to convey and express action as the logical development of incidents. Rather than his theories, it was the rich textures of Brecht's stage aesthetic and the clarity of his direction which drew admiration and influenced a clutch of directors and designers across Europe, including several who saw his work in Britain for the first time in the 1950s. The Berliner Ensemble became renowned for their immaculately physical and detailed interpretations, performances in which every actor had a refined sculptural quality no matter how small the role. Brecht's work brought 'a fresh sense of the stage as a space with a relationship to the audience... and he was able – like a really good screenplay writer – to introduce concepts into theatre not through talking about them, but by showing them happening, showing their effects.'[187]

'For me, Brecht is and still is much more fascinating as a great theatre director than as a playwright.'[188]

Peter Brook

Brecht's visual aesthetics focused audience attention by arranging and grouping characters to ensure the story and action of the play were crystal clear. Placing and attitudes of characters were considered carefully to draw attention to particular points of interest which fuelled the inherent debate of the play, its central core. Peter Hall points out that, 'if you achieve clarity on stage you actually make an audience understand the sexiness of argument, the sexiness of political argument, and that dialectic is actually theatrical.'[189] Brecht exploited theatre's ability to present two different things at the same time, promoting what Raymond Williams famously called 'complex seeing'. An example is when Mother Courage invites the Cook and Chaplain to join her behind the cart to discuss the progress of war with a glass of schnapps while her dumb daughter Kattrin dresses up in a pair of red boots left behind by Yvette the prostitute. As the audience watch Kattrin for several minutes (there are two pages of text at this point) they simultaneously listen to the conversation between Mother Courage and the men, absorbing two disparate things at the same time – one visual, one aural. While spectators can be entranced by Kattrin's behaviour they are not allowed to forget the circumstance of war thanks to the discussion behind the cart. In filmic terms, this would mean establishing the conversation behind the cart in one shot and then cutting away to Kattrin, so the political conversation would continue on voice-over on screen as we watch Kattrin's mime with the boots.

Thinking of the choreography in relation to cinematic shots opens up ways of exploring how the spectator's view of the action can be steered and focused. The assumption is often made that a theatre audi-

'I think that theatre has to embrace the vocabulary of its audience and the vocabulary is now that of film.'[190]

Robert Lepage

ence is in possession of a multiplicity of viewpoints simultaneously, and they have free choice as to where to look, whereas a film director decides on the degree of distance or closeness an audience have to the action or character via the camera lens, and this dictates what the audience see within each frame, whether it's a long shot, mid-shot or close-up, for example. In the late 1940s Arthur Miller was writing a screenplay, *The Hook*, set in the gangster-ridden world of the Brooklyn waterfront, which may well have influenced *A View from the Bridge*, not only in relation to the research he undertook on the dockside, where he first heard the story he tells in the play, but in the way he orchestrates the action. The way he writes the play directs the action in a filmic manner. The play opens with the equivalent of an 'establishing shot': the curtain rises to reveal the street and tenement block with the Carbone apartment occupying the main area, and the audience's 'camera eye' travels like a 'panning shot' to take in Alfieri's desk downstage and the two longshoremen pitching coins on the other side; when '*A distant foghorn sounds*', the cinematic feel is almost complete. Then Alfieri enters and '*The two pitchers nod to him as he passes*', creating virtually the equivalent of a 'mid-shot' momentarily punctuating another 'travelling shot' as Alfieri crosses to the desk, taking the spectators' attention with him, and where he '*removes his hat, runs his fingers through his hair*' – another mid-shot – before he speaks to the audience and breaks the frame. The stage directions are given an extra fillip when Alfieri asks: 'You see how uneasily they nod to me?', indicating Miller expects the audience to have seen that action. To show all this on film would require splitting the screen or dividing the shots to accommodate the different locations. Miller exploits the multi-dimensional nature of the stage by having everything happen simultaneously, directing the action so as to draw the audience in as though they *are* the 'camera eye'.

'Encourage, where possible, distance between actors, especially on open stages. This widens the angle of vision for the audience.'[191]

Alan Ayckbourn

Cultivating a cinematic approach and experimenting with the idea of using different 'shots' becomes a way of estimating the degree to which you can control the focus of an audience by seeing them as a potential 'camera eye', drawing them in to particular actions/moments/characters or drawing them back so they gain a wider perspective. Be warned, this is not composing for a camera lens and squeezing action into talking heads – far from it. The naturalist sensibility of an enclosed room with a missing wall neatly transfers to the small screen, particularly in soap opera and similar incarnations, with characters hemmed in and operating at close quarters, and where characters quarrelling on screen can be filmed so as to appear to be spitting words in each other's faces. With an open stage, one which invites spectators in while keeping them literally at arm's length in their seats, thinking of the spectators as though they *are* the 'camera eye', presents a very different proposition: here it is the distance *between* characters that opens up conflict. Space between them allows emotions to ricochet; it needs to be treated like an elastic band which can be pulled taut or allowed to relax, making players reach out emotionally over distance to their partner. This is what raises the emotional barometer.

What you need to keep uppermost in mind as you experiment is that 'the human eye moves faster and has a far wider range of vision than the average camera shot'.[192] So while physical distance between players on stage widens the field of vision of the audience, exploiting characters' relationships with space means playing the elastic, creating opportunities to draw the audience's eye to details, perhaps to focus on one character's reaction, or accentuate a moment by the geometry of placing and arrangement. This is the reverse of what seems the more literal realism we see on screen.

Scott Graham and Steve Hoggett, co-directors of Frantic Assembly, are pioneers of extremely vibrant popular theatre, who are hugely influenced by the form and techniques of film and music video. They confess to being

'We always try to imagine what will bring an audience forward in their chairs, and what will send them reeling backwards.'[193]

Scott Graham and Steven Hoggett

obsessed with 'using the stylistic devices and techniques of film-making and trying to create work on stage that embraces these practices.'[194] A particular 'golden rule' they have adopted from film in structuring stage work has been: 'When cutting from one shot to another, there should be a difference of approximately thirty per cent in terms of the framing of the shot... e.g. from a close shot to a mid-shot.'[195] This is similar to the notion of percentages referred to earlier in Section 4 and it is largely through playing with such contrasts that filmic effects can be engineered.

'In comparison to theatre, film will always be a greater influence on our work.'[196]

Scott Graham and Steven Hoggett

Making use of perspective, scale and pace are techniques to explore. Creating perspective creates scope for long shots, though it is worth bearing in mind that the longest trajectory on a framed stage is the diagonal and this line is generally more interesting visually than the mid-line from back to front stage. The mid-line was once considered the 'power-line', with the king traversing from back to front stage in proscenium configurations. The diagonal is considered more 'thoughtful'. On the limited space of the trestle stages of *commedia*, actors used the diagonal because it gave the longest trajectory, and gave them more opportunity to be acrobatic.

Bringing an actor closest to the audience, such as downstage, may seem the most obvious place to attempt the theatrical equivalent of a close-up, since we are used to close-ups dwelling on the face filling the screen, providing an intimate portrait of reactions which indicate the internal state of a character. However, considering what other people are doing on stage in order to direct the spectator's gaze is also an option. At its simplest, if everyone on stage looks at the same place or thing, the audience tend to look there too. This requires players to focus on one character and demands discipline from them; everyone works hard to serve that moment. Using a 'fixed point' for one still character in a highly populated scene while others scurry round is a rather less obvious tactic, yet steers the audience's attention in a different way, with a not dissimilar result more akin to those moments in film when the camera travels round a character at speed. Playing around with ideas and testing them out using other groups as an audience is the best way to proceed. The key lies in creating contrasts between one shot and the next via spacing or pacing, or by magnifying or reducing the lens through physicality, as a way of drawing the audience into significant moments.

Rather than attempting to replicate cinematic shots, it's about being inventive with what you have. The use of percentages is immensely helpful here. Can you do things in a very small way in the midst of some huge thing, allowing very small

'It's all about finding the focus in the scene. So if you want a close-up you have to focus on a particular place on stage.'[197]

Jane Hartley

things to be read in a very big way? Or perhaps if something very tiny and subtle is going on, then the next thing happens very quickly. You could bring everyone together and put them in a very small, tightly defined space; a couple of chairs create a door on stage providing a frame to squeeze into, for example. The next exercise invites experiments on the basis of finding shots.

Shot-by-shot

Work in pairs on a scene or scenic fragment that everyone is familiar with and divide up the script into cinematic shots. Decide on where the audience should be looking, and label each moment according to whether it is best suited to an establishing, long, wide, mid-shot or close-up.

Once each pair has agreed on the shots, they then work individually as directors with a group each, exploring the possibilities for composing the imagery in relation to the agreed 'shot sequence' in collaboration with the players in the group. If necessary, use a ten-word stripped text that the group can learn quickly rather than have players with scripts in hand.

Play both versions of the scene and discuss.

Although the variance in this work can depend on the scene chosen, what emerges are various creative solutions to composing the shots. And the exercise is a useful reminder of how important it is to remember the audience's visual perspective.

'During rehearsals you discover how many options there are for one particular moment (usually dozens) and then gradually narrow them down.'[198]

Alan Ayckbourn

When Miller was researching *The Hook,* he was working alongside Elia Kazan, who went on to develop and direct the iconic film *On the Waterfront* (1954) with the writer Budd Schulberg. Schulberg transposed the screenplay into a stage play. When Steven Berkoff directed this play in 2009, he shunned the naturalism of film. He used his trademark 'total theatre' to evoke the movie's atmosphere and environment with a chorus whose physical and visual language became virtual camera angles and zoom lenses, conjuring the equivalent imagery of film.

On the bare stage before a cut-out silhouette of the New York skyline and with the occasional use of a few wooden chairs, Berkoff's dozen-strong ensemble created the throbbing life of the Brooklyn dockside and its seamy working class. Spaced around the stage in the shadows they hummed the growl of traffic as the protagonist Terry Malloy 'drove' a car engineered from a couple of chairs; with their collars hunched up against the rawness of the riverside night, the chorus melted offstage as though into streets and alleyways as Terry courted the unions boss's daughter. One minute they were trilby-hatted union bosses, the next hungry dockers huddling round an imaginary brazier as they waited to be hired; piled round a traffic-cone-as-bar-table, they morphed into mobsters flicking through wads of dollars; in Terry

Malloy's pigeon loft, scrunched up on the backs of chairs, they pecked and cooed in a virtuoso display of bird mimicry. This description of some of the images from *On the Waterfront* indicates how the chorus operated in cinematic terms, demonstrating how an ensemble on stage can orientate and steer the audience's perspective through physical and visual means. In so doing they created arresting theatrical imagery.

> '*Berkoff created a coherent visual language that seems like the theatrical equivalent of the movie.*'[199]
>
> Charles Spencer

Berkoff is renowned for his use of mime with an ensemble to create psychological and physical environments, the inner and outer worlds of a character. In large-cast productions, chorus actors play multiple smaller roles, and when working with a smaller cast, as in *Greek*, they play both 'defined characters' as well as the chorus. On many occasions Berkoff has taken the central role himself, playing Hamlet, Eddy and Coriolanus and memorably using mime in his rendering of Kafka's Gregor as the man-turned-into-a-beetle in *Metamorphosis*. One of his signature techniques is slow motion, a device through which spectators are drawn in imaginatively. It is virtually written into the script in Scene Five of *Greek* when Eddy and the café Manager mime a fight in single words, with the other two performers echoing the actions and reactions rather like people watching a tennis match:

MANAGER. I'll kick you to death and trample all over you / stab you with carving knives and skin you alive.

They mime fight.

EDDY. Hit hurt crunch pain stab jab

MANAGER. Smash hate rip tear asunder render

EDDY. Numb jagged glass gouge out

MANAGER. Chair breakhead split fist splatter splosh crash

EDDY. Explode scream fury strength overpower overcome

MANAGER. Cunt shit filth remorse weakling blood soaked

EDDY. Haemorrhage, rupture and swell. Split and cracklock jawsprung and neck break

MANAGER. Cave-in rib splinter oh the agony the shrewd icepick

EDDY. Testicles torn out eyes gouged and pulled strings snapped socket nail scrapped

MANAGER. Bite swallow suck pull

EDDY. More smash and more power

MANAGER. Weaker and weaker

EDDY. Stronger and stronger

MANAGER. Weak

EDDY. Power

MANAGER. Dying

EDDY. Victor

MANAGER. That's it

EDDY. Tada

WAITRESS. you killed him / I never realised words could kill.

Greek, p. 116

'There is a strange similarity between the sportsman and the epic actor both of whom have to move with great precision.'[200]

Alain Gautre

Slow motion 'bends time'. Like a microscope it enlarges what's happening on stage and is a valuable tool for attaining precision in movement and actions. Applying the technique of a slow-motion replay to a scene which has already been action-scored or one where you have employed the framing device of cinematic shots brings key actions and reactions to the fore. There is an added frisson with a chorus working to enhance the visual image by reacting to what occurs to steer the focus of the spectators. Just as television slow-motion replays of match points or goal scores alert us to the key moments in a game, you discover what is essential and flag up where you need to pare away movement that is purely decorative and not serving the focus. Slowing actions down, even those as prosaic as the pouring of a cup of tea, can ritualise them. Actions slowed indicate something beyond the everyday. They can create very sensuous and mesmeric movement and achieve real eloquence purely through the body. And it can be quite surreal; theatre can operate like a dream and you don't have to work to create realistic portrayals: 'the way people move in a dream is quite normal by the standards of the dream.'[201]

Finding the most effective pace for actions in presenting scenes in performance is a later decision to be made when you are at the stage of reviewing them in relation to each other and, like silence, slow motion can very easily be overworked. However, it is a powerful rehearsal strategy to illustrate where imagery and focus need attention, where you realise the enormous discipline necessary in using the body with clarity.

Approaching scenes via specific incidents by working out ways of presenting the action visually and using differing levels of physical engagement pays dividends: you discover images and movement that bleed into the development of everything else. A play lives on in the memory of spectators through vibrant images, snatches of dialogue, vignettes, moments of intense emotion. During rehearsals what goes into each individual element is isolated and dealt with independently. In performance they coalesce.

'Theatre, first and foremost, has to be a poetic medium.'[202]

Steven Berkoff

Choreographing knowledge is vital for any apparent narrative; searching for the thematic, symbolic and empathetic serves metaphorical aspects of stage composition and dynamics. A multi-layered quality in performance calls for ambiguity without reducing the audience to a constantly singular emotional response. When physical and visual imagery augment the logic of plot and characterisation, an image structure reaches towards the poetic, working as a theatrical meta-language. As echoes and patterns in movements and gestures evolve during rehearsals they become visual motifs, developed into stage movement. Once adopted and refined, the impact of these penetrates the audience at kinaesthetic and sensory levels.

'I would never think of recreating pictures on stage, but paintings do inform my creativity.'[203]

Declan Donnellan

The process by which complex visual images are created is rooted in being imaginative and intuitive, but it also helps you cultivate a visual sensibility. Theatre directors frequently refer to art in relation to their work, and not only modern directors. When Max Reinhardt invited Edvard Munch to collabo-rate on a production of Ibsen's *Ghosts* in 1906, it was not just for the decor, as Munch 'made a series of paintings that would help the actors develop their understanding of their roles',[204] paintings as expressionistic as his famous *The Scream*. Graham and Hoggett describe themselves as 'Impressionists rather than Surrealists.'[205] Classes Littlewood drew up for her actors incorporated studying painters, including Bruegel, for example, and these studies of art fed into how they placed themselves on stage in relation to each other and the set. Bruegel and Bosch both influenced Brecht's visual aes-thetics, with their canvasses crowded with communities of individuals performing seemingly strange or vulgar actions with all the intensity and purpose of naturalness.

As well as being well versed in modern art, Beckett was steeped in the Old Masters. A painting by Casper Friedrich of two men gazing at the moon was an inspiration for *Waiting for Godot*, and the play is suffused with imagery from Western painting that amplifies the many religious references peppering the dialogue. When directing the play in Berlin in 1975, Beckett shaped actions to allow crucifixion imagery to flicker into life. The mention of two thieves either side of Christ was taken up visually at the point where Vladimir and Estragon consider suicide for the first time (in Act One, p. 19) with them standing separately with the tree-as-empty-cross/potential-gibbet between them. This image resurfaced when they held up Lucky between them (in Act One, p. 45), and again in Act Two when they held up the now-blind Pozzo (p. 84). In the 'pile-up' as Lucky, Pozzo, Estragon and finally Vladimir collapse in a heap (Act Two, p. 93), their bodies were placed in a cruciform. The crucifixion is an abiding image of suffering in Western art; having employed this at various points, the final image sees the two tramps at the tree with Vladimir's trousers round his ankles when he has removed the cord holding them up as a possible rope for the tree-gibbet, puncturing the potentially tragic with the farcical and simultaneously punctur-ing any suspicion of the play embracing Christian ideology.

Actively looking at paintings, sculpture and the way architects use space boosts creative resourcefulness, particularly in relation to working with space and considering the visual dimension from the spectator's perspective. Confronting canvasses of different dimensions has a profoundly different effect to viewing images through the frame of a computer screen where everything is minimised and equalised, so visiting the art gallery is time well spent. Scientific eye-tracking analysis of people's responses to looking at paintings show that solving visual problems creates a tangible response in the viewer. A distorted image actually creates pleasure, and the brain gets an extra 'kick' when things are exaggerated or out of proportion. Different neurons fire when looking at one of Picasso's Cubist paintings, for example, with the brain working out how to knit the full image together. The principle stays true for theatrical images, and there is an obvious correlation here between the notion of the 'grotesque', where opposites and visual distortions cohabit, and the idea of things out of scale mentioned earlier.

When you look at a painting with figures in it, you can see the relationships between them. A performance should try and make everything clear visually so that it tells as much of the story visually as it does verbally, if not more.

Section 6

Inside the Words

Inside the Words

The power of visual images can be enormously seductive, yet spoken words are no less magical, persuasive and highly active.

To treat any text, no matter how 'realistic', as poetry is to look for hidden meanings, allusions, sonorities, rhythms, and to refuse to take words at face value. Dialogue may be crafted to appear and sound like everyday speech but it isn't. That is an illusion created by the playwright. Like poetry, words in a play are shaped and honed to convey not only semantic meanings, but also nuances or ambiguities, to generate rhythms and cross-rhythms, patterns and symbols. Even in the most prosaic of plays, metaphors and leaps from one plane of thought to another are part and parcel of the whole.

'The best theatre thrives on a marriage of language and spectacle.'[206]

Harriet Walter

Several levels of meaning operate when words are spoken: sonic, rhythmic, dynamic and semantic. The sonorities of speech in tone, pitch and inflection register and connect with us. Vocal actions are as vital as physical actions. A range of detail and musicality is integral to the conviction and allure a character has for a spectator. How vocal and physical actions are calibrated is the challenge. Words provoke sensations and sensations provoke physical responses because speech is a physical act. Your voice is a physical instrument, produced inside the body and manifest as an extension of it. When spoken out loud, words act on the unconscious as well as the conscious; they connect to the characters' energy force fields, driving the play forward and unveiling its kernel. New discoveries surface when they are set free inside the body.

'The voice is an invisible body which operates in the space.'[209]

Eugenio Barba

A gestural approach pays attention to intuitive understandings, seeking life behind literal meaning to inhabit words at their root, feeling language in the body, music in the words in order to release their sonic and sensual nature, responding to the texture of rhythms and patterns with a 'constant respect for the internal dynamics of the text'.[208] This is as true for a modern text as it is for an older one.

Rehearsals with scripts in hand become mechanical and lack energy; very little can be achieved with a book or even a few photocopied pages in hand. The point at which explorations meet actually voicing a playwright's words is a tricky one and players are often reluctant to relinquish the script. They need to be alert and imaginative, watching, listening and responding – with both hands free. Keep texts nearby during improvisations and trust that players will gradually come closer to the actual words written, even if they have been paraphrasing up to this point. Simon Callow uses the analogy of 'defrosting' the words on the page. If you learn the words before getting to grips with the thought patterns, he says, 'you lay down rail-tracks which you must follow and any sense of the thoughts and impulses which gave rise to the words is very hard won.'[209] Memorising lines is best done by rote, learning them in monotone rather than attempting to 'act' them. Remember that line-learning is a gradual process; the key in committing them to memory lies in familiarity with what is happening in the moment, as action and ideas and thoughts intertwine. Character journeys chart their progress through the events in the play; how they speak is a kind of linguistic DNA, yet no matter how they speak, what they say begins as an impulse.

Language is structured, shaped and patterned to be inherently dynamic. However, the energy so apparent in making physical discoveries often dissipates

'We enter a text through the body.'[210]

Jacques Lecoq

when actors get to the point of speaking actual lines. We associate speaking with our head and brain at the top of the body since that's where both speaking and listening happen, something reinforced by a daily diet of headshots of actors and newsreaders on the telly. And because our eyes are the sense through which we apprehend the world we tend to focus on our head as the location of impulse and intent. Donnellan points out that, perhaps unconsciously, we think of energy 'trickling down from the brain' or 'radiating from the head' rather than 'welling up from the ground'.[211] His exercise called 'Ground energy' is an immensely valuable starting point to feel language in the body and access its energy. What follows is how I use it; it works well following a warm-up which ends in relaxing the body on the floor – players need to have a speech or some lines of dialogue already learnt.

Ground up speaking

Players lie down and relax, directing attention to the points of contact with the supporting floor. Make sure the knees are soft and the neck free as these are points where tension restricts the flow of energy necessary for freeing the voice.

Each player has several lines of text learnt, which can be a section of a whole speech or a few shorter lines – around five or six will do. Once everyone is relaxed, players begin speaking the text, letting it travel from the floor up through the diaphragm and into the lungs, and up and out through the mouth. Make sure the breath comes from the base of the lungs – and use one breath for each sentence.

Try this a few times so everyone gets the sensation of the words resonating through the body. Notice how the words seem to start in the base of the belly and rise up through the throat, which feels quite open.

Then come to standing and repeat the speech – think about it coming up from the floor and travelling up through the length of the body from the soles of the feet.

If you find the throat constricts when you stand, perhaps you haven't given the exercise full commitment when lying on the floor, or maybe you unconsciously hunch your shoulders when you come to standing.

A common anxiety is hearing your own voice, and tensions in the body can inhibit the full release of vocal power, particularly in the knee and neck areas. These need to be soft.

'No word is properly understood unless it has been spontaneously created by the imagination.'[212]

Declan Donnellan

To view plays as poetry in the Greek sense of the word, i.e. as construction, turns the lens to searching out the dynamics inherent in language through uncovering its sonic and rhythmic properties. If you treat heightened language like naturalistic speech you short-change the playwright and the audience. And if you treat naturalistic speech as everyday conversation you denude its vigour. However ordinary dialogue may seem, it is never totally naturalistic: 'it is a careful construction designed to appear naturalistic... For a start the balance of words within a sentence are carefully weighted.'[213] Apart from the occasional long speech, most plays operate through dialogue, which is artificial conversation, and what is said on stage is largely a response to what someone else has said. John Harrop is one of many directors who assert that intellectual understanding is not necessarily helpful to the actor's capacity to express meaning.[214] For it isn't always about meaning. There is, in the words themselves and their placing and rhythm, more to investigate than semantics. Poetry is dense and many-layered, designed to work on our sensory perceptions. This is relevant to any play, not just Shakespeare or verse plays. There are poetic qualities in seemingly realistic dialogue. Bond and Kane have a simplicity and brevity in the spoken exchanges reflecting the stark situations they conjure, lyrical in their abrasiveness, for poetry conjures the ugly as well as the lovely. The Soldier's speech from Scene Three of *Blasted* is an example:

> SOLDIER. Went to a house just outside town. All gone. Apart from a
> small boy hiding in the corner. One of the others took him
> outside. Lay him on the ground and shot him through the legs.
> Heard crying in the basement. Went down. Three men and four
> women. Called the others. They held the men while I fucked the
> women. Youngest was twelve. Didn't cry, just lay there. Turned her
> over and –

Then she cried. Made her lick me clean. Closed my eyes and
thought of –
Shot her father in the mouth. Brothers shouted.
Hung them from the ceiling by their testicles.

Blasted, p. 43

When we say a writer has a 'good ear' for dialogue, we don't mean
simply what characters say but the particular manner in which they
articulate their thoughts. So the 'inner ear' is not just inside of the
organ on the side of your head, but a deeper listening device to
apprehend and be alert to shifting moods expressed in the writing.
Modulations in key, register, harmonics, are all precise musical
indicators steering actor/singers in musical theatre or opera when
acting through song; in theatre, verbal texture and verbal shifts are
activating signals. As well as verbal imagery, changes in rhythm or
punctuation can indicate a change of thought, just as alterations in
cadence can signal a change of tone or timbre. Finding these out
isn't always helped by sitting
round a table analysing them
on the page. It requires listening acutely, not just through
the ears but feeling the words
through every fibre in the body.

*'The tool of intuition is more
subtle and goes much further
than analysis.'*[215]

Peter Brook

Sonic values

We have a subconscious response to language spoken and language
heard. There's intuition in our understanding of language which is
sometimes of more value than academic analysis. The reciprocal
relationship between players speaking dialogue is fundamental:
both speaker and listener discover a 'deeper "other" layer to its literal, surface meaning'.[216] We make subliminal connections in the
sounds themselves when heard and, for the speaker, as a result of
the body's involvement in saying them. For example, the expressiveness of swear words comes to some extent from their
plosive-ness; an internal energy generates emotional surges when
they're uttered and accounts for their forceful effect on those on the
receiving end.

At a sonic level, words are evocative. Babies respond to the tonal quality and rhythms of voices: the lilt of a lullaby or the curse of a cross parent elicit distinctly different reactions. And audiences derive pleasure from the aural qualities of words and their poetic and rhetorical arrangement, the weight and balance of their syntactical patterns. The sonic properties of words tap below and above the ordinary and everyday, reaching beyond the cerebral to offer sensual, visceral and spiritual dimensions of understanding, touching the inner ear. Linda Marlowe recalls how Berkoff's interest was often directed more at the musicality in the sounds of words than their meaning in rehearsals. And he always 'stresses the physical act of articulation and demands that actors give every word its full value, just as a musician has to strike every note'.[217]

You can, as Brook so interestingly discovered when working with the poet Ted Hughes on *Orghast at Persepolis*, find expression in the sonorous shape and pattern of words even if their meaning is obscure. In the act of speaking heightened language from atavistic texts and Ted Hughes's own invented language, actors communicated profound emotion without knowing the semantic meaning, powered inside by the sonorities and rhythms of words they uttered.

'Super-cali-fragi-listic-expi-ali-docious!'

Mary Poppins

We play with words as children, enjoying their oddities as much as their meaning. Who hasn't amused themselves by saying a word like 'banana' over and over again in different rhythms until it loses all sense and becomes just a jumble of syllables, almost sound-music, and collapsed giggling? Games with words free players from having to make sense of them, allowing them to explore what language provokes; how words feel on the tongue, in the mouth and in the belly; what makes us feel upbeat or downbeat. Remember this is not simply frivolous – the games *are* the work, and exploring a play's peculiar music through trial and error can be fun as well as serious. Once playing becomes the focus it gets rid of the idea of 'doing exercises' and can reap equally fruitful benefits. Injecting laughter into a line, even when the line is serious, or injecting a catch of breath, is a game that works well in pairs, with players trying to outdo each other to see who is most pleased with themselves at each attempt. An element of competition seems to remove inhibitions if they are invited to select each other's best attempt, which can then be replayed to the group and one voted 'bestest'. The by-product of this is that players pay more attention to how they use their breath in delivery, and how crucial it is in creating emotional effects.

Speaking lines learnt and practised can often feel calculated rather than spontaneous. The director Katie Mitchell finds that getting actors to run round the room shouting can often liberate the material. And concentrating on another task or playing a game while speaking allows the conscious brain to take a back seat; focusing on something else releases rhythms and inflections so words adopt different patterns independently. This is what Cicely Berry calls 'displacement activity' and her game Jostling, where players form a close group and jostle one another, works to benefit either an individual speaking one speech or several players with dialogue from a scene. The instinctive annoyance at being jostled feeds into the player(s) speaking so that expression becomes more forceful. The game also frees the voice since vigorous movement in the body causes the voice itself to loosen up and find new pathways, forcing words to erupt in unexpected ways.

There are a number of games and exercises for physical approaches to text in the final section of *Through the Body* called 'The Physical Text', and rather than repeat those here, what follows are additional and more detailed.

Rhythm

Words and their rhythms work on us like music, setting up vibrations that evoke more complex meanings than rational thought might yield. Rhythm works on us at a subconscious level. We're aware of this in how music or drumming prompts dance when our feet tap almost automatically and we feel beats flow through the body, or how an increase in BPM in electronic music raises our heart rate. Spoken language is similar. From the moment of

'The rhythm of language affects us in a very deep way.'[218]

Cicely Berry

birth a baby responds to the rhythms, patterns and intonations of the mother's mother tongue absorbed during gestation. Whether the mother is Chinese or French, it is the beats and intonations of her voice the baby recognises. This may explain why 'we understand something through rhythm which may be outside our full literal comprehension'.[219]

The language used and its verbal texture is unique to each playwright. Sound, rhythm and meaning are interrelated and there is a particularly intense inner connection between them in Shakespeare. Beckett's work is often described as musical with its inbuilt rhythms and word-music. *Waiting for Godot* was originally written in French, Beckett's second language; the resonances of his Irish lilt live on in the rhythms and cadences of his English translation, and these were also engagingly well-suited to the West Indian accents of the black British cast in Ian Brown's production with Talawa in 2012. Beckett's language is as richly condensed as any poet's, deceptively familiar in a context in which any everyday utterance is enhanced by the charge of the situation. It is playful, superficially absurd at times, yet although Vladimir and Estragon are placed in a surreal situation, a place of pure theatrical imagery, they refer to ordinary things we can identify with.

Berkoff's sinewy language is elaborate, mask-like in the way it distances from reality while at same time offering a heightened reality, yet still rooted in the familiar. He attempts to redefine the relationship between the physical nature of performance and the literary nature of a play. His linguistic vulgarity is playful and the vibrancy powered by images ripe for physicalising: in *Greek* the density of Eddy's speeches look like daunting soliloquies on the page, but embedded within them is a choreographic score for the chorus. The rhythms are full of syncopated beats that feed into the shaping and pace of the visual images. The language directs the imagery.

'You have to create the music which is in the text: there is no orchestra behind you.'[220]

Annabel Arden

The energies found in uttering lines allow words to vibrate, to provoke sensations in us. There is a pulse even if there is no verse metre, a pulse which has to do with balance and weight.

The word-music of *Saved* is stark and unmelodic, the line lengths at times almost uniform in Scene Six, creating a steady rhythm that inflects the gradual cumulative build of the actions. What the original director, William Gaskill, calls the 'flint-like stops' of the short sentences in *Saved* accentuate the apparent banality of the dialogue and the inarticulacy of the characters, a kind of inertia framed in staccato beats. In *Top Girls*, the impression is of fast-moving conversations, with the overlapping dialogue generating urgency and attack. There's vigour in Miller's *A View from the Bridge*, in the harnessing of the Brooklyn longshoremen's accents, contrasted with the slightly halting Sicilian accents of the immigrants.

Whether verse or prose, the arc of meaning in speech, long or short, is governed by punctuation, and its emotional life is bred in the impulses of the actor. The way sentences are structured, whether short or long, or even a single word, is a guide to the rhythm of speaking; punctuation is the clearest aid to exploring rhythm. A sentence – or phrase if bounded by a full stop – is an active unit and, 'The movement of a sentence is the same in verse or prose.'[221] It is the journey of the thought that governs this movement. Phrasing by punctuation serves the meaning, even when that meaning may seem obscured by long-forgotten vocabularies. A simple exercise to get this idea lodged with players is for a groups to learn one speech – around six to ten lines will do – and then all speak it together while stamping their feet for a full stop, clapping their hands for a comma. Invent your own body percussion for other kinds of punctuation, such as dots and dashes.

A move in the midst of speaking usually indicates to the audience there is a change of tack or a shift in a character's thinking. In sailing, tacking is a term used by sailors for zigzagging across water to catch the prevailing wind to move forward. This next exercise exploits that idea. It is based on 'taking a sentence for a walk', a common technique employed by voice coaches. Everyone uses it in their own particular fashion, so this is my version. Each player needs several lines, either from a speech or from a scene where a character has lines of dialogue that have been learned, and make sure players know where the punctuation occurs – it's essential to be accurate with this. Rather than work with the script in hand, put it somewhere close by in case anyone needs to check it.

Sentence tacking 1

Pick one sentence and speak it without stopping for any commas, semicolons or dashes – don't stop until the full stop – while walking purposefully, neither rushing nor dawdling.

Start another journey with the next sentence if using a speech to work on, or the next sentence from the same dialogue sequence. By all means 'hear' the other character's line in an exchange to get the sense of what prompts the next line – and 'mark time' at those points.

Now fix a point opposite where you're standing, something at head height, like a light switch on the wall. Walk the next sentence as you did the first, but now direct the new sentence to that spot.

Continue in the same fashion with the next sentence and so on.

Reflections on the exercise so far:

- Notice whether the pace of walking changes with each sentence.

- Do you overrun the distance to the point on the wall? Is this because you walked faster than the distance you allowed?

- Do you stop short of the distance to the point on the wall? Is this because you have a short sentence or because of your pace?

Repeat the speech and, each time you rerun a sentence, experiment with judging the distance between you and the point on the wall and monitor what happens when you reach it at the full stop, and what happens when you don't.

Then repeat the exercise ensuring you change direction with each stop this time, using a deliberate turn to fix a new point somewhere else in the room for the next sentence.

This gives a physical sense of the relative fluency and flow of lines. Players get some indication of how active thoughts are, how pace affects these and alternative options for delivery. There's a sense of discovering thoughts as paths through which you travel. Using a speech from a modern play offers insights into the rhythm of the whole speech as the difference in sentence length becomes transparent, like the one from the Soldier in *Blasted* transcribed earlier, where a single comma and two dashes reveal those momentary interruptions in his train of thought: these are there too for the audience, giving them a moment to absorb the impact of the tale he recounts.

Once players have got the hang of the exercise – it takes several goes – move on to the next version, dealing with interior punctuation.

Sentence tacking 2

Use the same speech extracts used in the previous exercise.

Now do exactly the same as in the previous exercise but change direction with every instance of intermediary punctuation, i.e. any commas, semicolons, dashes, ellipses.

NB If there are long sentences and lots of punctuation, players may need to keep the script held in hand for consultation to begin with; once they've had a few goes at this they find they know which words precede and follow the punctuation.

Players may find this quite challenging and frustrating since the thoughts they were getting hold of through the flow of the sentence are broken up, and the rhythm feels disjointed. The less punctuation in a speech, the more the thought pattern has clarity; the more punctuation the more the thought pattern seems interrupted. This is more likely to arise in older plays as modern playwrights tend more often to write in shorter sentences. In the latter half of the twentieth century, sentences got shorter, less rhetorical and more ambiguous. In the twenty-first century we are accustomed to the way lots of short thoughts are expressed in short, clipped sound bites in the media, which is how Ian and the Soldier speak in *Blasted*, and, since we're unused to reading hefty novels where writing is packed with images and thoughts mulled over and considered from numerous angles, we may struggle with sentences that seem, to the modern ear, of unusual length. The tacking exercise is about finding the rhythm through walking the words, a physical activity to locate the verbal shifts that indicate thought patterns.

One of Donnellan's exercises takes the notion of a sentence walk and augments it for working with a Shakespeare speech. A player crosses the room to touch the wall on the last word at the end of each line of a learned speech. If in a small room, walk, if in a big room, run or skip. As the exercise continues and is repeated, the player becomes more astute at judging the pace required to ensure s/he touches the wall only on the last word in every line. 'The exercise helps the actor to see the time a line may take and to feel that verse springs as much from the body as from the head.'[222]

Tackling the rhythm via punctuation is quite technical. Rolling a tennis ball across the floor and speaking the text until the ball stops concentrates on the flow of a speech in a more meditative way. Vary the amount of pace injected into the roll. Here the trick is to try and imbue the delivery with the motion of the ball, depending on the speed it travels. This gives a different sense of the speech travelling – this time outwards. It's almost as though the ball carries the words.

There are two essential human rhythms, both of which relate to our emotions: our breathing and our heartbeat. In order to deliver verse, particularly

'The verse gives its energy to the actor.'[223]

Declan Donnellan

Shakespeare and Berkoff, attending to the breath becomes a necessity because the sentences are often longer. Berkoff employs oblique dashes to indicate the rhythm, and the implication is that delivery goes at a cracking pace. The punctuation in Shakespeare is often disputed by academics who doubt the prompt copy or print-setter's ability to place it correctly. Try reading Shakespearean verse without punctuation and it shows how much breath is necessary. A lot. Just as physical precision has to be nurtured so does breathing. Chopping up verse into bite-sized chunks that don't require lung capacity and controlled exhalation is not the answer – doing this will tame the energy within it when what's needed is finding the energy to fill out the speech. Tackling such verse requires training the breathing to accommodate speaking the full length of the thought.

Shakespeare is often considered the most verbal kind of theatre and the pinnacle for actors. McBurney describes Shakespeare as 'most physically present' and advises: 'Don't act... find the musical rhythm first and foremost... then you can find the dramatic shape and the emotion at the heart of it.'[224] There are numerous approaches and many manuals on speaking Shakespearean verse, and those of Cicely Berry and Barbara Houseman offer actors exercises that help to find the musical rhythm. In verse, the shifts of gear are like modulations in music, flicking from major to minor, becoming suddenly percussive or undulating as though surfing waves. The basic iambic rhythm is close to ordinary spoken English and based on the rhythmic beat of the human heart. It's quite easy to replicate the rhythm in everyday conversation. Try spending breaks in rehearsal speaking only in five-beat lines – get everyone to count the beats on their fingers to begin with. 'Would you like a coffee or a tea?' is a common example. It may seem a trifle weird to start with but players soon become accustomed to it and relish the task and, of course, enjoyment always brings confidence.

'Once you learn the rules you chuck them out of the window.'[225]

Judi Dench

Peter Brook warns against viewing the iambic pentameter as a set of rules. Declan Donnellan points to the practical difficulty for modern actors: 'the length of thought demands far more breath than the actor needs for most modern texts'.[226] The most succinct advice I've come across is the section at the end of Donnellan's book *The Actor and the Target* where, in twenty-odd pages, he dispels many myths and provides pragmatic suggestions for individuals to find their own way, forged through his experience of working with actors from many nationalities, and illustrated by dissecting a speech from Shakespeare's Juliet. While the best way to build affinity with verse is to read masses of it aloud, the other necessity is to learn and practise breathing to manage longer thoughts.

Unpicking the meaning is not to be neglected, but the way through is often less about the semantics of individual words and more about the rhythm of the whole. A grasp of the persuasive powers of rhetoric may be of more value than a glossary when it comes to many plays, including Shakespeare. There is a formal pattern in the lines which you ignore at your peril. This is not simply the metre. The rhetoric has to be played – and this is built on opposites moving towards a conclusion. Rhetoric requires a sense that the speaker is leading to a conclusion, with phrases building on one another towards some kind of resolution. Words and phrases are balanced to unleash an underlying debate. The following line from the chorus in *Antigone* illustrates this in a highly compacted form, where the alliteration and repetition support the rhetoric in a short phrase and a short sentence:

Savage child of a savage father. Suffering has taught her nothing.

Antigone, p. 19

When Stephen Fry first encountered *The Importance of Being Earnest* he was left 'simply boggling with excitement. I had never heard language used in such a way, had never known that the rhythms of a sentence could be so beautiful... I had never known that writing could do more than tell a story, that it could excite in the way that music does.'[227] Wilde's language has musicality of a different kind to Shakespeare's, with rhetoric evident in the highly structured wordplay. In the tea-party scene between Cecily and Gwendolen, dialogue builds through repetition with both saying the same thing in different ways. Once the niceties are out of the way and they get down to the business of arguing about who is engaged to Ernest, their catfight is embedded in rhythmic patterns:

CECILY (*rather shy and confidingly*). Dearest Gwendolen, there is no reason why I should make a secret of it to you. Our little county newspaper is sure to chronicle the fact next week. Mr Ernest Worthing and I are engaged to be married.

GWENDOLEN (*quite politely, rising*). My darling Cecily, I think there must be some slight error. Mr Ernest Worthing is engaged to me. The announcement will appear in the *Morning Post* on Saturday at the latest.

CECILY (*very politely, rising*). I am afraid you must be under some misconception. Ernest proposed to me exactly ten minutes ago. (*Shows diary.*)

GWENDOLEN (*examines diary through her lorgnette carefully*). It is certainly very curious, for he asked me to be his wife yesterday afternoon at 5.30. If you would care to verify the incident, pray do so. (*Produces diary of her own.*) I never travel without my diary. One should always have something sensational to read in the train. I am sorry, dear Cecily, if it is any disappointment to you, but I am afraid I have the prior claim.

The Importance of Being Earnest, p. 55

All the stiff-upper-lip and epigrammatic expression is mask-like in offering a heightened reality with an exaggerated archness overlaying any deep emotions.

Dynamics

'It's a question of physicalising things and making action very clear.'[228]

Annabel Arden

Verbal shifts in words and their sequences conjure intuitive responses on an emotional level. Decisions made about the emotion of a speech before digging into its form and rhythms tamper with the range of expressiveness demanded. Overemphasising feeling 'makes the language passive'.[229]

The effect of speaking words in the moment, when working in a space with fellow players, is very different from reading them alone or collectively. Nuances and contradictions emerge through speaking which develop and augment the work on characters. Dialogue often crystallises the core of a conflict, and players respond physically to the images, rhythms and the internal dynamics. Once aired, words can surprise both the speaker and the listener, allowing meanings and feelings to shift in the responses between them. Words work on us and in us. When spoken aloud they feed our unconscious physical responses; speaking becomes dramatic because of the effect it might have not only on other characters or events but because of the change occurring inside the player speaking them.

The next exercise illustrates this in practice; as it relies on familiarity with cane dancing from p. 101 of *Through the Body*, that exercise is repeated here with slight adjustments.

Cane dancing

Use long bamboo canes (two metres) for this. Lay one cane between two players. They should stand a couple of metres away from the cane and make eye contact, then walk towards it. Keeping eye contact, they pick up the cane at the same moment and balance it between them using only the flat tip of the middle (longest) finger. It is now balanced precariously between them. As they move around, the cane remains supported between them until one of them drops their end. Use all of the space right to its limits.

You can play this as a competitive game where the aim is to make your opponent drop the cane by forcing them into awkward positions. The 'dance' will be over quite quickly.

However, if you resist the competitive urge and try keeping the cane supported between you for as long as possible whilst aiming to make your partner be the first to drop their end, the 'dance' becomes more intricate as you both find more and more subtle ways of outwitting each other – using levels such as going up on tiptoe, twisting under the cane, moving backwards and sideways, as well as pushing forwards. In soccer terminology, you are playing the ball not the man.

This game explores the chemistry between players to energise movement in a light and dextrous manner. Play the *Cane dancing* first so that players get the hang of the game before moving on to the next task – one which has never failed to produce results from workshop participants. This next exercise is designed for pair work, so cast players as two characters in a scene or use players already cast in a scene between two.

Stripping the text 2

The ten-word scenes from the previous version of this exercise in Section 5 (see pp. 104–105) can be utilised if appropriate, or generate a new ten-word script for a scene between two characters. Look for key words that capture the reactions of the characters in the scene to convey what is happening. Once the text is stripped down to ten words exchanged between the characters (i.e. maybe five each, maybe 7:3 or variances depending on the scene), learn those words as the script for this exercise. You can also try it with a speech directed at a character who doesn't answer back, so that all ten words are spoken by one of the characters – this will force the non-speaking character to respond without words to what is being said.

Use the bamboo canes as in the previous exercise.

As the cane hovers between the players – as they 'cane dance' – they find moments to utter the words in the ten-word script. The dance energises speaking born from the attempts to keep the cane in play, which can become quite strenuous. It's important to have room to travel the space and use it to its fullest extent to avoid merely going round in circles or back and forth. As players continue repeating the ten-word script as the text, they discover more and more alternatives in delivery depending on how the push-and-pull of the cane dance progresses.

Once they have explored the impact of playing the cane dance with the ten-word script, players then learn the actual dialogue and cane dance while speaking the actual lines.

This generates an instinctive feel for the emotional significance underpinning a dialogue exchange. Players have to focus on each other and consequently pay their attention outward, adding to a real sense of a relationship between characters, their feelings towards each other and the situation. The energy of the cane dance injects urgency into delivery and gives a strong sense of an internal dynamic. Making dramatic language active relies on playing tension between characters to locate the intensity of expression, and *Cane dancing* exposes the push-and-pull dynamic of the mental and emotional actions between characters. Once the scene is played without the canes, players tend to have a more spontaneous feel for movement and gesture, and their reactions attain a more convincing depth. A valuable by-product of this exercise is how it cements lines as players tend to be more accurate afterwards.

'Speech and the very nature of the text change according to bodily tension.'[230]

Jacques Lecoq

Conflict in drama is not always full-blown but simmers under the surface, and *Cane dancing* with a stripped text physicalises those tensions. Reactions are key, and since 'playing the reaction to a line, a thought or a feeling is much more difficult for most actors than transmitting',[231] the benefits are for both parties. The resistance felt in keeping the cane balanced provokes a need to react, even if you have no lines. For individual speeches, using another player pushing against the speaker provides resistance; as the player speaking pushes back something releases in the mind and the body – words erupt as though it 'cost' something to produce them.

Dialogue is a two-way process in which the push-and-pull dynamic of action and reaction is embedded. Characters use words for a purpose. They are bound up with intent. Intention is about expectation and the future, and the concept of push-and-pull can be useful in activating a sense of being compelled/pushed-or-pulled to do something via a physical impulse, or repelled/pushed-away/pushing-away to resist doing something. Finding the push/pull dynamic in the ebb and flow of dialogue exposes underlying tensions between characters but can also be accessed by individual players. Because within every action lies a counteraction: within any choice of what to do lies a rejection of other options. The exercise *Playing drunk,* towards the end of Section 2: Serious Play, generates a sense of an interior push/pull dynamic which offers a physical sensation of the emotional riptide that is a counteraction. And *Animal on a lead* in Section 4 does something similar. Replaying these can help players find the physical embodiment of counteractions.

To be active, words need to be filled. Playing with them not only makes words more sonorous and searches out rhythms but familiarises you

> '*What we say is about who or what we are speaking to.*'[232]
>
> Declan Donnellan

with what characters say. Working on the inherent dynamics in dialogue, as in the last exercise, turns attention to what the words are doing in terms of the story. The words themselves are an active force, so it's necessary to play what the words actually *do* in terms of affecting other characters as well as expressing thoughts.

The mantra for playwrights is 'show don't tell'. Steve Gooch advises anyone writing a play: 'What characters say to each other in dialogue is less important than what they're doing with their dialogue.'[233] Characters attempt to alter the perspective of others. Exercises in removing or reducing the text (as in *Stripping the text*) force players to search for actions and gestures to render the situation, and find the energy in uttering the written words. At a semantic level, the meaning of dialogue is informed by the intention behind the lines.

The tone of speech is just as significant as its content. Think of how you use your voice to convince someone to do something or give you something, how you use a different tone to warn someone or flatter, coax or threaten or tease them.

Caryl Churchill's *Blue Kettle* is a short play which illustrates how the total impact of a play is far more than the spoken words. It tells the story of how a man and his partner con elderly women into believing he is their long-lost son. Once the situation is well-established so that the audience are aware of the con-trick being played out, Churchill begins replacing key words in the dialogue with the substitutes 'blue' and 'kettle'. An early example is where Derek introduces his girlfriend Enid to Mrs Oliver, one of the elderly women:

> DEREK. Mrs Oliver, I'd like you to meet my friend Enid.
>
> ENID. Nice to meet you Mrs Kettle.
>
> *Blue Heart*, p. 53

Superficially and taken out of context on the page this looks potentially like comedy, with Enid appearing as though she's got the name wrong, but because the substitutions occur periodically and with all the characters – and the dialogue is played absolutely for real – the audience register that this is a kind of game, and take it seriously. Initially 'blue' and 'kettle' crop up intermittently in a rather arbitrary fashion at points where it is obvious what they stand for, as in the example above; as the play progresses they gradually appear more and more often. This may seem bizarre, yet an audience simply works out what is happening, the action and relationships and how the plot unfolds, so that meaning is utterly unambiguous. Once the audience recognise the game the playwright is playing, they simply go along with it. Derek comes clean when he visits his real mother in hospital:

> DEREK. My kettle is to trick the blue kettle out of their money. My girlfriend doesn't like it and she might blue me. I'm not sure I blue enough to stop kettle it. Her name's Enid like Enid Blyton. I've told you that before a blue kettle.
>
> MOTHER. Oh yes we like Enid Kettle.
>
> *Blue Heart*, p. 60

Eventually sentences might contain several 'blues' and a couple of 'kettles', and towards the end of the play, even these are truncated to 'bl' or 'ket'. Because the context is crystal clear, and the actors play the situation and speak the dialogue to all intents and purposes as though they are saying what they mean, an audience has no problem following the narrative.

What this illustrates is not only Churchill's playful mastery of dramatic writing, but the way dynamic structure organises how situations and passions are played out in communicating meaning in a play. Using words other than the semantically correct ones does not inhibit meaning. Action, reactions and interaction, tone of delivery and demeanour of the players are a primary channel through which meaning travels.

What characters hope to gain or dread losing is embedded in what they say and how they say it. There are many alternatives, possible ambiguities and angles to try out in saying the lines. It is possible to convey numerous inflections on a line to convey different meanings. Playing the alternatives and gradually narrowing them down is the way forward before making a decision about which of them is most effective once you know the situation.

Words contain actions

'Action is inscribed into words.'[234]

Jacques Lecoq

The agendas created by the dramatist, whether conscious, semi-conscious or hidden, relate to a character's function in relation to the plot, fuelling actions and reactions. When the agenda is conscious, characters tend to say what they mean. At other times they may say one thing and mean another. As Gaskill reminds us, 'Any line in a play is said by a character in a situation and is not a statement of objective, scientific fact... it may have more than one meaning but it cannot have an infinite number of meanings.'[235] A familiarity with the shape and action of scenes from workshopping them means players already have a handle on what characters mean when speaking. The extent to which their agendas are displayed in dialogue lies in uncovering the needs of characters, short term or long term, which leads to unveiling intentions.

It was Stanislavsky's analytical insight that characters pursue what he called an 'Objective': they want something, and their journey through a play is a series of actions through which they attempt, not always directly, to get it. The idea of character having a 'want' is especially valuable when we remember its other sense: to 'be wanting' is to lack something. There may be something the character doesn't have that they want, as in the case of Macbeth, who wants the crown, and then when he gets it fears he might lose it, and so everything he does once he's King are strategies to ensure he keeps it. You cannot play an objective, only the actions that might enable a preferred outcome to materialise.

'The transitive verb is a conduit and vessel for energy.'[236]

Steve Waters

Most actors are aware of the method of 'actioning' a script, often accredited to the director Max Stafford-Clark, but also familiar to other actors and directors, and borne from seeking out what characters *do*, actions designed to achieve a desired outcome. Actioning a script involves establishing Stanislavkian objectives for a scene and dissecting individual lines: actors cast in role use a transitive verb to describe what the character they are playing is attempting to do with each line, depending on what they want to achieve. In this systemised process, lines are transposed into phrases – e.g. *'I persuade'*, *'I flirt'*, *'I resist'* – and these are written next to the line of dialogue in the script. This method attempts to fix actions via analysis prior to full explorations in space with other actors. It offers 'great value in terms of clarity of thought,' the actress Kathryn Hunter found, although 'if used too early on in rehearsals it blocks'.[237] And she points out that a player's relationship to the play tends to be with a book rather than their partners. Rehearsals using this system can become very static initially, and, since it relies on actors having extensive vocabularies in order to particularise the intentions of characters from a psychological perspective, some actors can feel inhibited. The focus is on ascertaining what characters are thinking and then translating it into activity or gesture. If players find themselves standing round in the middle of a scene debating which action is best, you're in trouble. They need to be testing out the alternatives rather than discussing them. So selecting transitive verbs as homework to bring to the rehearsal floor is perhaps one option.

In his book *Different Every Night*, Mike Alfreds gives detailed instructions of how to apply actioning through testing various alternatives in a Chekhov play, through an organic process tackled physically rather than intellectually, since actors' bodies are sensory. He warns against playing the result of an action instead of embodying it as an activity sensed within the body. William Gaskill points out that despite its many virtues, actioning can inhibit a discovery of how an objective might flow through a sequence of exchanges and, 'it doesn't probe the intention of the action, it only describes the action itself.'[238] Many actors find it a useful method if they are stuck in generalisations and need to be more specific, particularly in trawling the subtext of a naturalistic play if the prioritising of psychological reasoning has shifted the focus away from the situation to character.

Bear in mind that characters frequently operate in exceptional circumstances, not always of their own making, and may well behave uncharacteristically, so it is not always apparent why they do what they do. Additionally, their actions may be designed by the playwright to show more than an illustration of human behaviour. Their dilemmas can be demonstrations of more than psychology.

Playwrights choose words, their placing and shaping in sequences, very carefully, and we do their play a disservice not to recognise the potency of this in relation to what a play is about. The words chosen serve the central core of a play and the

> '*Sometimes [characters] say things that I don't necessarily quite know why [they] say them, but I know they have to be said.*'[239]
>
> David Hare

linguistic singularity of characters, as well as the story. Language is functional at a deep level. While words operate in establishing situations, delineating and revealing characters and propelling the story forward through actions, they also conjure the world of the play and capture its thematic concerns. What characters say relates to ideas outside their individual predicaments, vibrating strings of intellectual ideas, images and social commentary alongside expressions of feeling. Politics, religion, cultural, moral and ethical positions, resonate in the words spoken. Through what characters say, a dramatist invites an audience to consider ideas and concerns sitting in the heart of the play. The words are a way in to the 'big ideas'. Searching these out is a level of activity as vital as searching out the actions and images, thoughts and passions inside the words.

'All playwrights think deeply about language and its functioning.'[240]

Steve Waters

The centre line of a play emerges from being alert to the specificity of the dramatist's choices. Like Beckett's 'themes of the body', verbal images and linguistic connections echo and reverberate through the lines. The kernel of a play can be located in a centre line bubbling up. For example, the centre line of *A Midsummer Night's Dream* is 'love', the word so often repeated to give every variation and mood associated with love, alongside the stories of love in the three worlds of the lovers, Oberon and Titania and the mechanicals' playing of *Pyramus and Thisbe*. It is not only verse plays that play with language in this way.

The complex conversations in overlapping dialogue in *Top Girls* operate on a number of levels. Embedded in the dialogue of Act One are snippets of factual and fictional perspectives on a range of

'Words tell us not just about the characters, they frame for us the political context of the play.'[241]

Cicely Berry

topics, from life in ancient Japan to European theology and the Victorian lust for travel, punctuated by the earthy pragmatism of Dull Gret's outbursts. The domestic concerns of women from differing cultures and epochs surf the waves of what appears to be dinner-table conversation, each a shifting viewpoint of women's lives. When we arrive in the corporate environment of Marlene's advertising agency in Act Two, more limited frames of reference percolate the speech of the aspirational women in the workplace. In the final act, Churchill throws us into the bear pit of a sibling argument where the sisters bruise each other in words. Here the device of overlapping lines injects urgency and, in the rapidity of exchanges between Marlene and Joyce, words seem to arrive before thought, powered by entrenched attitudes. For an audience it is as fiery and absorbing as a tennis match. This is not merely a family argument but a political debate too. The impulse driving the words is not pure familial resentment. What they say embodies the adage that 'the personal is political'. If we admire and aspire to have Marlenes in boardrooms, the cost is borne by the Joyces.

A play has words in the script that are not dialogue, unspoken but nonetheless vital, and it is these I want to turn to in the next section.

Section 7

Around the Words

Around the Words

The previous section focused on working through the words to be said. Aside from these and those relating to settings and design, there are words that describe actions and objects which become instrumental to the image structure of a play.

Stage directions

'For me the language of theatre is image.'[242]

Sarah Kane

Stage directions perform similar functions to dialogue: embodying action/moving the story along/revealing character/referencing themes. The degree to which playwrights separate them from dialogue ranges from Kane's explicit images, the fulsomely detailed and precise instructions of Beckett and the emotionally charged directions of Miller, to the meagre offerings found in Shakespeare, Büchner or Berkoff. It seems that most of Shakespeare's plays were compiled from prompt copies with directions largely confined to entrances and exits, occasionally supplemented by additional instructions: by and large directions are implied in the dialogue. This extends to a level of detail in characters' reactions, so for example Barnado's line to Horatio: 'How now Horatio? You tremble and look pale', indicates the physical reaction of the actor playing Horatio in response to the appearance of the Ghost. And of course much of the dialogue of any play has similar directions inscribed in the spoken words. However, separated written directions open up avenues of enquiry in just the same way that the words characters speak open up sources for imagery and action. The examples cited in this section demonstrate a variety of ways in which they operate, and the importance of paying close attention to them as stimulants for interpretation.

'Every action on stage is in some sense symbolic, from killing a king to pouring a cup of tea.'[243]

William Gaskill

A poetic symbolism emerges when Bond's stage imagery is realised and made concrete. The directions for Harry's entrance to Len's bedroom in Scene Twelve, following the attack on him with the teapot by Mary, read as follows:

The door opens. HARRY comes in. He wears long white combinations. He wears pale socks. No shoes. His head is in a skull cap of bandages. He comes up behind LEN.

Saved, p. 107

On stage he resembles a ghost, a dreamlike figure appearing as Len pokes a knife through the floorboards to better hear the sound travelling up from Pam's room below. The resonance of this image goes beyond the ostensible realism of the situation, stirring something in the spectators. Similarly, in the final scene of the play, Len is draped over the seat of the chair he is mending with one arm dangling, an image Bond has stated is drawn from classical Greek statues depicting attitudes of grief. The ambiguity inherent in this image provokes questions rather than providing a single resolution or answer; it has been described by some commentators as an image of optimism and by others as one of acceptance. Because the final scene takes place in silence (there is only one line), an audience are involved on two levels: waiting for someone to speak and trying to absorb what the image might be saying.

The visual is as important as the verbal in Beckett, and his stage directions are meticulously placed. What is seen and what is done are as vital as what is said, evident in instructions which are as considered as every

'Beckett has changed the way we act, the way we write and the way we direct in theatre.'[244]

Peter Hall

word to be spoken. The repetitions and patterns of movement specified are integral to the image structure of the play. Fastidiousness in following them geometrically and mathematically determines the precise execution of the visual iconography on which his plays depend. For Simon McBurney, 'This does not feel any more of a restriction than the words you are required to speak. Quite the opposite. Its precision is an injection into the artery of the imagination.'[245]

To '*remain motionless, arms dangling, heads sunk, sagging at the knees*' as in the following extract, creates memorable sensations in the bodies of those performing as well as a highly potent image for spectators. Just playing the directions in this extract without the dialogue creates a sequence of physical actions that convey a considerable amount. In playing Beckett, the 'knowledge' is so often in the choreography:

VLADIMIR. You'd make me laugh if it wasn't prohibited.

ESTRAGON. We've lost our rights?

VLADIMIR (*distinctly*). We got rid of them.

   Silence. They remain motionless, arms dangling, heads sunk, sagging at the knees.

ESTRAGON (*feebly*). We're not tied? (*Pause.*) We're not –

VLADIMIR. Listen!

   They listen, grotesquely rigid.

   Hssst! (*They listen.* ESTRAGON *loses his balance, almost falls. He clutches the arm of* VLADIMIR, *who totters. They listen, huddled together.*)

   Sighs of relief. They relax and separate.

ESTRAGON. You gave me a fright.

Waiting for Godot, p. 19

In this extract the relationship between Vladimir and Estragon becomes tangible in gestural acts demonstrating their similarities and mutual dependence. Here we find Beckett's 'themes of the body', that phrase he used to describe creating patterns in gesture and movement that would register with the audience. Repetitive symmetry in patterns of movement emerges as these recur at various points throughout the play. Yet variation is important. Beckett insisted the first time a gesture is performed it should be done in an unusual way to alert the audience to it so that subsequently the audience really notice it: 'When in a text actions are repeated, they ought to be made unusual the first time, so that when they happen again – in exactly the same way – an audience will recognise them from before.'[246] This is a strategy for unlocking the image structure in the text that keeps an audience engaged through visual choreographic details.

As a director, Beckett concerned himself with the balance and rhythm of organising gestures with the same precision as the words. He asked for movement to be 'balletic' to capture the physicality he required from actors. And here we are in the realm of theatre with dance at its centre. In this respect his aim resonates with Artaud's desire for theatre to be 'poetry for the senses'; he grasped the singular expressiveness of gesture and mime.[247] His lifetime appreciation of silent movies and love of Keaton, Chaplin, et al. is not only apparent in the vaudeville routines in *Waiting for Godot*, but also indicative of his understanding of the complexity involved in mime and gesture. He saw mime as a tool for the actor in much the same way as Lecoq.

His notion of 'themes of the body' is extremely valuable as a technique for developing significant physical attributes and emotional attitudes in characters. Searching these out in any text flags up points where audiences will recognise character and action through the body. Think of how visual gags in comedy work on spectators when reappearance of a gesture or look is the trigger for laughter. In dramatic plays, the mechanism is similar although the outcome is not a laugh.

'If you cry, the audience will not. The actor must exercise restraint.'[248]

Peter Hall

Miller's directions in *A View from the Bridge* trigger layers of meaning in the actions to be played. Clues to physicalisation abound in Miller's stage directions, charting clear emotional journeys for characters. Looks and glances feature often, adding subtextual signals to actions embedded in the lines. As we saw with the opening of this play, there's a strong similarity to screenwriting, and throughout the play Miller invites gestures that sum up a character's feelings at particular points, sometimes in small behavioural ways such as Catherine '*clapping her hands together*' at the news that Beatrice's cousins have docked (p. 5), at others with an accompanying metaphor for the emotional context, as when Beatrice tells Catherine she needs to 'act differently' around Eddie now she's a 'grown woman' and can no longer throw herself at him like a twelve-year-old:

> BEATRICE....Just give him to understand; you don't have to fight, you're just – You're a woman that's all, and you got a nice boy, and now the time came when you said good-by. All right?
>
> CATHERINE (*strangely moved at the prospect*). All right... If I can.
>
> BEATRICE. Honey... you gotta.
>
> > CATHERINE, *sensing now an imperious demand, turns with some fear, with a discovery, to* BEATRICE. *She is at the edge of tears, as though a familiar world has shattered.*

A View from the Bridge, p. 33

Rather like Beckett's precise patterns, these directions render clarity in the relationship between characters, for, although so very different a play from Beckett's, Miller's directions are similar in how they provoke physical reactions. Played as written they provoke sensations to guide emotional inflections. Just before Eddie Carbone play-fights Rodolpho in the boxing lesson at the end of Act One, the direction reads that '*he pulls his trousers up over his belly*' (p. 43), and he hitches them up again in Act Two (p. 70) when he is bruising for a fight with Marco. Before that first trouser-hitching Eddie has been '*unconsciously twisting the newspaper into a tight roll*' in response to the information that Rodolpho not only sings and makes dresses but also cooks; a few lines later '*He has bent the rolled up newspaper and it suddenly tears in two*'. The energy required to tear a rolled-up newspaper is intense, prompting physical sensations in the person playing Eddie – the tension elicited shows Eddie's internal anguish through the body. Gesture and emotion are two sides of the same coin, and the alchemy that occurs in the body transmits to the audience.

With great plays it is not just what is put in the mouths of actors that matters but what they put in the heart and the body. Situation brings this alive. Reactions occur not only in relation to other characters but to strategically placed events. Exploring and experimenting physically with actions and gestures provoke sensations which travel like lightning through the body and produce

> '*Movement must be utilised to express something significant for the action.*'[249]
>
> Bertolt Brecht

feelings. A famous example is Helene Weigel's silent scream when Mother Courage hears the shooting of her son Swiss Cheese. She has just sent Yvette off with a message to tell the Sergeant that she will pay the two hundred to release her son after all towards the end of Scene Three. As she sits waiting with the Chaplain the sound of drumming is heard in the distance, signifying the firing squad. As the drums ceased the actress arched her upper torso backwards and opened her mouth wide without emitting any sound. A spectator described the impression on the audience: 'It was the sound of absolute silence. A silence which screamed and screamed throughout the theatre, making the audience bow their heads.'[250]

When her son's body is then brought in on a stretcher and the Sergeant pulls back the sheet asking Mother Courage to identify it, the directions state simply that she shakes her head. Gaskill recalls the fixed rictus smile on Weigel's face as she made very slow progress across the empty stage to look at the body of her son. Once she turned away from the soldiers after shaking her head to deny she knew him, the smile disappeared as the muscles in her face dropped.[251]

> '*An actor's special gift is the ability to resist, to hold back, to tame, to keep energy in, to concentrate.*'[252]
>
> Anne Bogart

With outpourings of grief we are left appalled and often embarrassed rather than moved. Yet we are moved by someone visibly suppressing tears. Holding a moment in a physically awkward manner in theatre creates an impression of emotional restraint, as in Weigel's pose where her spine was contorted and her neck muscles tightened to hold the head back, stiffening the whole body to project intense emotional power. The facial contortion of her rictus smile combined with the slow movement across the stage work in a similar manner. When the normal balance of the body is dislodged it exerts an effect on those watching, the inner tension in the dynamic of the actor transmits visually to the spectator. This is most obvious if performers appear to be in a potentially physically dangerous place, such as balanced precariously, as in circus when we see acrobatic feats with high levels of physical risk. When what's on stage has an element of risk related to the emotional situation of characters, audiences identify with the threat they face in a similar fashion. Frantic Assembly regularly exploit this, presenting highly energised, deft choreography to reflect emotionally charged situations for characters. It is worth noting that investing emotion in a Frantic show is left until later: only towards the end of the rehearsal process does movement become 'infused with emotional meaning of character or relevant performance instinct'.[253]

Restraining passion lies at the heart of embodiment. The stage reality of emotion is different from life reality. In stage reality, emotions need to be transformed by constraint and shaped by judgement to affect an audience. Certain emotions tend to be associated with familiar actions, such as wringing hands for despair, or punching the air for joy; it is easier to slip into cliché, harder to resist the familiar, and when actors use well-worn clichés an audience struggles to take them more than superficially. Feeling is bound to well up in players at points of emotional significance. It's part of the job of the actor to deploy these in order to move the audience. Donnellan uses the analogy of a tube of toothpaste: the feeling may be fulsome but expression is more powerful when squeezed through a small aperture. When a turbulent scene makes you feel emotional the actor William H. Macy's advice is to 'put a lid on it, get the job done, and the audience will fall apart.'[254]

A physical gestural language that moves, disturbs, or even wounds the spectator conveys what characters may be feeling but do not articulate in speech. The difficulty is gauging

'The physical situation [has] to reflect the emotional situation.'[255]

Scott Graham and Steven Hoggett

whether what you are offering the audience is something new or whether you are patronising them by stating what they have already deduced. When Graham and Hoggett of Frantic Assembly commission writers, they are looking for opportunities for physicality which they regard as having what they call 'space' to express in the choreography what is not said verbally. The 'unsaid' provides 'rich pickings for choreographed physicality,' because for them, 'the subtext is crucial'.[256]

A common danger lies in finding emotion in the character and applying it willy-nilly rather than drawing emotion out from individual
situations presented. In a German production of *Saved* the actress
playing Mary had decided the character was 'angry' and applied this
by banging the tablecloth every time she laid the table, an invention
based on her conception of the character. But the surprise and power
of the moment when she snaps and hits Harry with the teapot is
completely undermined if Mary is played with her emotional dial on
'anger' throughout. The incident with the teapot is an unusual occur-
rence; it took twenty years to make her finally snap.

> *'It is the audience who must feel, not the actors.'*[257]
>
> Simon McBurney

If, as the director Ariane
Mnouchkine suggests, 'the
actor's body can only perform
when an author gives him material that comes from the
heart',[258] it is important to recognise a dramatist's heart is motivated
by more than sentiment. Brecht's much-vaunted concept of a character's *Gestus* invites actors to make imaginative use of the wider
social-political perspective of the world of the play in figuring out
Stanislavskian given circumstances. In the Berliner Ensemble's production of *Mother Courage*, Ekkehard Schall performed Eilif's war
dance in Scene Two as though this was a young man who had been
taught the ceremony, with his head tilted and 'lips pursed as though
in an effort to recall the next movement'.[259] In doing so, he showed
Eilif does not own the dance but simply does it because he thinks it's
the right thing to do. Similarly, the actress playing the Peasant's Wife,
who kneels and prays when her son is taken away by soldiers in Scene
Eleven, knelt and prayed in the original production in a way that
showed for someone in her situation this was 'what people did', that
praying was a ritual undertaken by someone numbed by constant
war rather than an outpouring of personal grief, that the Peasant's
Wife does not own the praying – she simply does it because it's
become the norm. The notion of psychological motivation is com-
pounded by the social circumstances of her life. An audience is
invited to see past the personal emotional circumstances and recognise the impact of social and cultural conditioning. This is where
Brecht's *Gestus* and *Verfremdungseffet* hit home.

Perhaps because of their political similarities, Bond is frequently allied to Brecht's proselytising. This is a misconception. 'Drama teaches nothing', said Bond in a recent interview, 'I hate all this Brechtian rubbish.'[261]

'The eye is not stupid – the eye sees socially – dramatic truth comes out of facing the paradox of a situation.'[260]

Edward Bond

He aligns himself more closely with the Greek dramatists and, like them, confronts spectators with situations that present moral and ethical problems, situations prompting difficult questions. The baby-stoning scene (Scene Six) of *Saved* is one. Trying to work this scene by ascertaining the motivation for the gang is a cul-de-sac. Instead of looking for conscious or deliberate motives founded on psychological reasoning, physically playing out the actions by 'finding the game' of stoning the baby is more enlightening. The gang need a level of exuberance and a sense that they relish the competitiveness of the game; the stones have to be thrown accurately so that they hit the target of the pram at the right moments, yet 'safely' so as not to fly into the audience or hit another character. Players have to figure out precision and detail in stone-throwing once they have found the game of hitting the target. Only when they can hit the target as indicated in the directions and dialogue can they really work on developing the looks and gestures between them around the words.

Kane does something quite unique with directions in *Blasted*. Her Author's Note states: 'Stage directions in brackets ( ) function as lines.' Speaking these bracketed directions puts the focus on a very precise playing of the situation. It's a useful restraint as it reminds players to separate or isolate those specific actions, making them distinct from the dialogue and the non-bracketed stage directions, rather than merging them into a generalised soup of action, speaking and gesture. By and large these bracketed stage directions draw attention to actions, gestures, looks, laughs, and interactions with objects, as though a camera is picking up on each one – each image quite distinct from the spoken dialogue. The following examples are from the first scene, so the effect on the audience is surprising:

IAN. I've shat in better places than this.

   (*He gulps down the gin.*)

   I stink.

   You want a bath?

CATE (*shakes her head*).

Blasted, p. 3

*

IAN. Your mother I feel sorry for

CATE. Like wh– what?

IAN (*looks at her, deciding whether or not to continue. He decides against it.*)

   You know I love you.

CATE (*smiles a big smile, friendly and non-sexual*).

Blasted, p. 5

According to Simon Kane, this differentiation between lines spoken between characters and actors speaking the directions was the playwright's intention. While speaking the directions may not be an instruction to voice the lines in a performance, doing so can be a production choice, and he states 'it may be perfectly valid to speak the stage directions, but that's a production decision.'[262] A diverse array of techniques has been employed to articulate these bracketed stage directions in productions: they have been voiced over through loudspeakers, spoken by a fourth actor on stage, written out and projected onto a backcloth. However, because speaking stage directions forces a separation of actions from dialogue and aids the development of precision and clarity for the audience, it's a strategy worth adopting during rehearsals for any play if you find everything is getting rather muddled. And speaking the actions you create as directions is another valuable strategy when there are none written, especially if you use the third person, as this helps clarify what you're doing and focuses attention outwards. This is especially helpful when dealing with objects.

Objects

Clarity of narrative and theme, feelings and attitudes of characters, poetry of metaphor, sociopolitical nuances, all these

'An object or prop visible to the audience must have a purpose.'[263]

Steve Gooch

extend not only to individual players and their interactions but also to whatever else is on stage. A play's image structure embraces everything on stage as well as actions and gestural language; interactions between characters and objects, characters and sounds are there to serve themes and narrative, carry meanings and resonances which all build into the matrix of signs the audience absorb in performance. Real objects and sounds demand integration into a rehearsal process just as mimed objects and live sound effects, whether those are literal or metaphorical renditions of what is indicated in the script. As with stage directions, exploring their significance opens up avenues for interpretation and conveying meaning(s).

There are several key objects used as narrative devices in *The Importance of Being Earnest*. A forgotten cigarette case of Jack's, inscribed with the name of his ward Cecily, is a plot device Wilde uses to amusing effect to set up the confusion over names and let us know that his pseudonym of Ernest is a ruse for his exploits in London. Jack's confession that he was a baby found at Victoria Station in a handbag when he asks Lady Bracknell for Gwendolen's hand (Act One, p. 21), is a classic example of an object used as a 'plant and pay-off', for at the end of the play the bag is retrieved and revealed as belonging to Miss Prism, Jack's one-time nanny and now Cecily's governess, who mistakenly put baby Jack in the bag instead of her self-penned novel and left it at Victoria. Objects can be valuable stimulants for finding games. The point when Algernon holds onto Jack's cigarette case begs for a chase, and Harrop suggests a game of tag 'to open up numerous patterns and choices but keep the playful energy of the scene'.[264]

'For me the objects I use are like words on a page. The way they are integrated makes them articulate.'[265]

Simon McBurney

When objects are active agents in the telling of the story, they become virtual catalysts, as does the love juice in *A Midsummer Night's Dream*, applied by Puck to the wrong lover. The teapot in *Saved* is functional for most of play, providing a seemingly innocent symbol of working-class life, until Mary smashes it over her husband's head in Scene Ten, when it takes on all the resentment and disappointment of their long marriage. The chair Harry then stumbles over as he attempts to retaliate becomes the central focus of the final scene, where Len attempts to mend it.

Objects are assigned values by dramatists, and we do well to consider what those might be. They are not simply decorative. Like words, objects have semantic values, symbolic and thematic values, emotional values and values assigned to them in relation to characters, and they become active elements on stage, often acting as contrasts. Pam's obsession with the *Radio Times* is manifest in the relationship she has with it, a distraction from what an audience might think are more important things like her baby; she watches telly rather than communicate. Pozzo has his pipe, vaporiser, chicken, etc., and whatever else might be carried in the bags Lucky shoulders, all the accoutrements of wealth; Vladimir and Estragon have only the odd carrot or turnip.

Object lesson

Grab a few highlighter pens and mark where objects are mentioned in the text, either in the stage directions or referred to in what is said.

What purpose do they serve?

Try figuring out the function of objects in relation to themes as well as characters.

You can chart the journey of objects in the same way as characters, combing the script for places where they appear and are used or referred to. Thematic values operate at the level of detail in the presence and use of objects and ways they contribute to the visual imagery; registering the way they are used in relation to the narrative is one aspect, discovering how they relate to the central core another. Macbeth's hallucinatory dagger contrasts with the actual bloodied knives he brings from killing Duncan, its illusory nature all the more significant when Banquo's ghost appears and when Macbeth revisits the Weird Sisters in Act Four and is faced with an array of surreal figures conjured by their magic. In *Woyzeck*, Marie's shard of broken mirror epitomises the poverty of her circumstances in stark contrast to the sparkling reflection it gives to the earrings she has been given by the Drum Major. Coffee in the office contrasts with tea in Joyce's kitchen in *Top Girls*; it is Marlene who can afford wine and whisky. The Sergeant's little book in the opening scene of *Mother Courage* establishes the fusion of war and business in the military, picked up by the use of the regimental cash box as a key plot device, and Courage undoubtedly counts the coins in any of her transactions. The significance of the newspapers in *Blasted* becomes apparent during the course of the play; the directions state in the opening scene that '*Ian throws a small pile of newspapers on the bed*' and then later in Scene Five when Ian is at his lowest ebb they read, '*Ian shitting. And trying to clean it up with newspaper*'. Kane said herself in an interview, 'From the moment he comes in and throws them on the bed we have to follow those newspapers right the way through – they have their own story in there, because that's what they're full of.'[266]

As visual components, objects trigger responses in spectators. In some plays they need to be real, as with Bond's teapot and Kane's newspapers, and mime is more suited to others, such as Berkoff's *Greek*. Used in a gestural manner, objects can transform, accentuating the metaphorical nature of the stage, as in Complicite's work where the flapping pages of books became a flock of birds in *Street of Crocodiles*, and in *Lucie Cabrol* planks held up by performers became the walls of the house, planks they banged loudly when the couple inside made love as though the house itself shook. Objects which stand in for the presence of something can carry as much if not more conviction than the thing itself. In *Mnemonic* they needed to represent the 'ice-man', i.e. a five-thousand-year-old-corpse found on the Alpine glacier in 1992, and since 'literal representation would be more than faintly ludicrous' they used a chair, 'but the chair was more evocative if broken, so we used a broken chair.'[267] The function of objects becomes active on metaphoric and emotional levels when explored in a dynamic way in rehearsals and can provoke responses that lead to powerful, potent images. In Richard Eyre's production of *Hamlet*, Hamlet threw Ophelia's letters in her face in Act Three, Scene One, then, as Claudius and her father Polonius emerged from their hiding place, she was scrabbling round on the floor 'gathering up the letters as though they were the shards of her life'.[268] In this production Ophelia's flowers were a bunch of black twigs, and she gave Claudius a gnarled stick on the line 'here's fennel for you and columbines'. In a recent production at the Young Vic, which set the play in a mental asylum, Ophelia handed out pills in stead of flowers.

Objects or props should never be left until technical rehearsals; it is preferable to find what you need early on in the process so you get used to working with them, or use appropriate substitutes. Even in the presentation of a scene or extract for peers, it is wise to ensure players have practised using any necessary items. There is nothing worse than being presented with items of food to be eaten, liquid in a cup previously empty, or a new item to incorporate into a scene during the final rehearsals. Players' attention is focused on dealing with the challenge presented by such items rather than involving themselves in performing with them.

> *'We always work with real costumes and real objects from day one. You evolve the whole thing, it's organic.'*[269]
>
> Annabel Arden

Locations

Like objects, anything deployed as setting has to have purpose and needs to be integrated with all other elements. That 'anything' means just that. Using objects to play with ideas for minimal setting can create imaginative solutions. Chairs are impressively chameleon-like. In addition to any number of different ways of sitting on them, playing with them to create and transform space and environments makes use of something that is usually easily available. The lighter the chair, the better, obviously, and risk assessment is a necessary precaution before you launch into playing with them. In the Sadari Movement Laboratory production of *Woyzeck* (adapted by Do-Wan Im, a graduate of Lecoq's), actors used ten chairs in ever-more intricate rearrangements to transform the stage in abrupt half-minute blackouts: the space became a cage, gravestones, a circus ring and a towering tottering frame which conveyed Woyzeck's crumbling inner turmoil.

As stated in the introduction, it is beyond the parameters of this book to engage with set design. However, pointers to design inevitably appear in stage directions related to settings, so some attention needs to be paid to them in that capacity. Playwrights sometimes incorporate ideas that present themselves as design problems, yet these can, and should, be addressed in physical theatre by working with the players.

'The play's world is discovered rather than created, found rather than imposed.'[270]

Declan Donnellan

Locations offer different energies, and the work on space and environment in Section 3 laid a foundation in using unencumbered space; when players successfully embody the environment a transformation of place occurs in the minds of audience. Actor-centric work thrives on minimal scenic decoration and working on an empty stage is a fruitful way to discover the need for any absolutely essential items. The less in the space, the more imaginative solutions you find. When there is less on stage to distract an audience, the more their attention is directed to the action. The limited funding available to Cheek by Jowl in their early years encouraged a pragmatic theatrical philosophy and a design ethos which necessitated anything on stage had to be multipurpose. Thirty years later they are still committed to that: in their 2010 production of *The Tempest*, a single wooden pallet on stage served as the only item on which someone could sit as well as for several other purposes, including upturned as a washstand; when Prospero set Ferdinand the task of moving the logs, Ariel became the logs, carried or rolled across the stage in various ways and, once parked on the opposite side of the stage, got up to run back round in place for Ferdinand's next trip.

Complicite employ an environmental approach to design that evolves during the rehearsal process. And the staging evolves in tandem with this as design materials and

'Metaphor and imagination are the poetic renderings of the real event.'[271]

Steven Berkoff

items are brought into the rehearsal space. You can work effectively through improvisation with everyday items to create the atmosphere of places. When creating the environment of a train station for Dürrenmatt's *The Visit*, Complicite actors would spend an hour or so on generating effects to give the sense of a train passing, such as working with a newspaper to shake it in the rhythm of the train approaching, swishing past on the 'platform' and disappearing down the track to convey the impression of being at the station.

For Berkoff, the idea of a 'set' represents what he sees as the barren imagination of directors, so his preference is for what he calls 'streamlined theatre'. Minimal set elements invariably controlled by the actors feature in his work, as in *The Trial*, where actors manipulated steel frames as doors, and as metaphorical cell bars to underline the mental torture of the main character Franz; sticks and poles were used for battles in *Agamemnon*. His work depends on mime rather than using props. Although Berkoff's *Greek* is located in London in the 1980s – specifically Tufnell Park – it is set on a bare stage with only a table and four chairs. In addition to using actors as a chorus, Berkoff is referencing the stage of Sophocles' original by stating that the 'three square and one upright panels' defining the stage area should indicate 'Greek classicism'. The play moves swiftly between the streets and pubs of the locale, Eddy's home and the café owned by his birth parents, and then on to the cave of the Sphinx. There are scene demarcations, but these are more to do with time than place, since locations change within scenes. There are no props: everything is imagined via the gestural skills of the performers, whose faces are whitened like mime artists.

As with objects, imaginative solutions can be as serviceable and even as powerful as the real thing. *Waiting for Godot* unfolds in a kind of nowhere-but-anywhere location that is irreducibly just the stage. But it becomes a physical world with its path traversing the stage, its stone and its tree, things we are actually familiar with in the natural landscape. Various attempts at putting a recognisable tree on stage have been attempted in productions around the globe: a lemon tree in Cyprus, an olive tree in Mexico, for example. The first production of the play was in a pocket theatre on the left bank in Paris. This was a 'low-budget affair' and the tree was constructed from coat hangers and cardboard, a curious sort of made-up realism like that created by children when they make a play in the front room and invite family and friends to watch. Lucky's suitcase was found in a skip by the husband of the theatre's cleaner.

'If you want to put anything on stage it's got to earn its place.'[272]

Declan Donnellan

When plays do dictate the use of furniture, only the bare essentials are necessary. Placing items to represent furniture can convey a place instantly, but it is frequently the space between blocks or chairs that indicates the environment. *Top Girls* can be staged with nothing more than a table and a few chairs placed in different configurations to denote restaurant, office, kitchen, and under which Angie and Kit can make their den.

Saved moves between the domestic realm of Mary and Harry's house and the public park, with additional scenes in Fred's prison cell and a local café. At the beginning Bond states: 'The stage is as bare as possible – sometimes completely bare.' Stage directions indicate a couch, armchair, table and TV in the living room at the opening, and a bed in Scene Five, although none of these is simply for decoration, and each item is used and becomes integral to the action. Even in this seemingly realistic setting, blocks, chairs and a table serve the purpose and can be removed between scenes when not required. When Fred sets out his fishing tackle and rod (bamboo canes work well here) on an empty stage, it becomes obvious where he is; canes can also act as oars. And once a balloon is tied to something like a chair rack or an office chair on wheels, it can serve as the pram in rehearsal.

Blasted has more spectacular effects, but a studio presentation using blocks can readily achieve these with imaginative minimalism. Place also determines and affects behaviour. Cate's awe at the posh hotel and the items in it is the sole focus in the opening scene of the play, bouncing on the bed and touching things, and summing it all up with a smile and the word 'lovely'. We take in the surroundings with her while at the same time noticing the fact she is unused to staying in such places. Certain locations breed protocols and rituals that we recognise. Dramatists not only use these to 'set the scene' but disrupt them to create disorder or shock. In this play, the pristine bed is soiled by Ian's rape of Cate before 'the arid security of that hotel room in Leeds is annihilated, as if the heath comes to Lear, with Ian sinking into a set shattered by an unexplained explosion.'[273]

The limited space in the Carbone's apartment in *A View from the Bridge* has the impact of characters being thrown together in close proximity. Limited space acts like pressure cooker, intensifying actions and moves that are circumscribed, with characters confined and possibly stifled. Defining the space for places as in the *Huge and tiny* exercises in Section 3 goes some way to realising the contrasts between big and small spaces, such as those in *Woyzeck*: Marie's room oppressive and small because she and Woyzeck are poor; the wilderness outside the town open and bleak. But it is players' movement and mood that establish places securely in the mind of the audience: 'The projection of life must be magnified to suit the optics of the theatre, not muted to reveal the subtext of reality.'[274]

While *Cane dancing* employs and exploits larger spaces to discover choreographic potential between players and gain a purchase on the physical relationships underlying the text, a similar result can be obtained by using the following exercise for a scene between two players working in a limited space. You need a long scarf made of sturdy material, or, if you prefer, a length of thick rope about three to four metres long.

Scarf duet

Players hold each end of the scarf/rope, and as they play the scene take it in turns to control the other player by tugging on their end to pull the other player towards them, reeling it in and/or letting it play out as they move away, finding the urge to do so in the impulses felt speaking the lines and playing the actions.

Once again the push/pull dynamic operates to inject movement in space and fosters a physical rendering of interactions at an emotional level.

Silence

In theatre, silence is shared between stage and spectator. In movement, silence beforehand focuses the attention on what is about to happen (as hushed spectators wait for first serve in

'Silence is loaded with different qualities according to whether it begins or concludes an action, an act, a word.'[275]

Jacques Lecoq

a tennis match), and silence afterwards on what has just happened. Like stillness, silence can frame actions, rouse our curiosity or tell us something. Not doing is not inactivity; silence is as active as words and movement in creating tension. Why has the playwright not given someone words? Or what is behind the choice not to speak? Silence on stage is compelling with characters who are actually mute, like Lucky (for the most part) in *Waiting for Godot* and Kattrin in *Mother Courage*. Their actions become magnified by virtue of their inability to speak.

Like stage directions, how much playwrights use silence or pauses varies. *Waiting for Godot* splices silence with speaking in deliberately crafted patterns, and Beckett himself remarked when writing it, 'silence is pouring into this play like water into a sinking ship'.[276] Noting where silence and pauses are written as directions may not simply relate to the intensity of moment between characters, it can also be the dramatist's cue for the audience to absorb something significant, perhaps in relation to its theme. This is evident in *Top Girls*, which is a very busy play where talking is virtually ceaseless. In Act Three, where Joyce and Marlene engage in an argument of unbridled sibling animosity, there are two stage directions for silence. The first (p. 76) follows Angie being bribed to go to bed with the promise that Auntie Marlene will come up, marking an anticipation point where an audience wonder what will happen next. By this point, the genie is out of the bottle, and, while the question of whether Marlene ever has done the bedtime routine might resonate in the quiet, it also gives the audience a breathing space to digest the accumulation of information and put two and two together. Marlene breaks that silence with a phatic remark about the weather: 'It's cold tonight.' The second one (p. 86) follows a political argument, signalling the audience to take in and absorb the differences witnessed between the two women. Marlene also breaks this silence in a line that is the nearest she comes to apology – a trite summary of a Thatcherite position:

> MARLENE. I don't mean anything personal. I don't believe in class.
> Anyone can do anything if they've got what it takes.

There are only four pauses in this act, and the first (p. 69) marks a moment of anticipation before Marlene articulates what the audience are wondering:

> MARLENE. I did wonder why you wanted to see me.

Two pauses (p. 81) frame Joyce's revelation that she had a miscarriage when Angie was six months old and Marlene's retaliatory revelation that she has had two abortions. These are clear markers to allow the audience to assimilate the thematic debate of the play. The other one follows Marlene's pseudo-conciliatory remark that she will stop talking politics:

> MARLENE. Come on, Joyce, we're not going to quarrel over politics.
>
> JOYCE. We are though.
>
> MARLENE. Forget I mentioned it. Not a word about the slimy unions will cross my lips.
>
> *Pause.*

Top Girls, p. 84

'Silence is as real as noise.'[277]
Peter Brook

Steve Waters advises playwrights that silence should be used with restraint: too much or too little and your audience is lost, either in their own world or in pursuit of recapturing yours. Churchill is a good example of this. Brook also advises restraint: 'one of the rules of silence is that it cannot go on too long'.[278] However, rules are made to be broken, and Edward Bond breaks this one quite spectacularly by creating a whole scene in silence at the end of *Saved*. Initially Gaskill delayed rehearsing this final scene thinking it was unfinished because of the lack of dialogue. It contains only one line of dialogue when Len asks for a hammer. Apart from this, detailed lines of physical actions in stage directions give a meticulous account for each character: Len's attempts to mend the chair; Mary's toing and froing from table to kitchen with the plates – presumably from a family meal; Harry searching for a pen to fill in his football coupon; Pam's page-turning with the *Radio Times*. Pam turns the pages of the *Radio Times* three times, a seemingly innocuous direction which, when played in the context of a completely silent scene acquires considerable weight. To work on the intricacy of these – how does Pam turn the page, when, and how long between turns? – creates a mesmerising effect. Stage time virtually marries real time. It's as precise as Beckett. There is a potency to rhythm whether in speech or action, and in this case it is the rhythm of the actions conducted in silence that draws attention and elicits concentration in onlookers. Bond has written time for the audience to reflect, exploiting the current of exchange between stage and spectator.

Silence is allied to shaping and pacing, which is where I want to turn attention to next.

Section 8

Shaping and Pacing

Shaping and Pacing

In performance, a play exerts power over an audience not only in relation to its genre, narrative, characters, and the production aesthetic, but through its inner rhythm. As discovered earlier in Section 2: Plays and Audience, this relates to how its structural layers reside in the unfolding of the play in time.

There is often a 'lift-off' point, usually about fifteen to twenty minutes in for a full-length play, a moment when, as an audience is pulled in, everyday life melts away as the imaginative world of the play takes over. Towards the end things reach a different gear, not always increasing to create intensity, sometimes slowing during the latter stages, but nevertheless, there is a strong sense of coming to the end of a breath. In the interim, we are bound up with the flow of the action embedded in the play's rhythmic score. Whatever the style of a play, whatever the manner in which it is staged, this flow of impressions is like a spool unrolling; a pulse beats with varying levels of intensity, each line or image a trigger for the next, right up until the final moment.[280]

'Theatre is in essence about time and rhythm.'[279]

Annabel Arden

Rhythm can make or break a performance. Simon Callow suggests that our sense of the length of a performance is related to its rhythm: 'if it seems over in a second, it was probably very good. If interminable, the chances are that it never hit its proper rhythm.'[281] When the rhythm is too regular the effect on the audience can be soporific. When the right variation in rhythm is struck, the attention of the audience is sustained. This is far more dependent on inner intensity than accelerating or decreasing tempo. As in music, tempo is simply the geometrical timing; rhythm is more elusive because it's organic. And it is through working with music that players' instinctive sense of rhythm can be enhanced.

Working with music

Theatre can be musical without being a musical. Caryl Churchill has said she often listens to the same piece of music at her desk, and what she writes takes on a tenor from that piece so that it becomes part of the DNA of the eventual play. Music works on an audience at gut level. The right music at the right moment can make a production soar. But music isn't only there to enrich a play in a decorative sense. Working with music is favoured by many theatrical innovators, and is integral to the work of many of the companies and practitioners whose ideas inform this book, whether they use it as an active partner in structuring or inspiring rehearsals or an eventual element in shaping a performance.

'I dream of a production rehearsed to music, but performed without music.'[282]

Vsevelod Meyerhold

For Meyerhold, the most important attribute in stagecraft is what he termed the 'gift of rhythm', a gift enabling a performance to be musical without music being played or sung. An accomplished violinist himself, he understood how time is sensory for musicians. He believed actors should be taught to feel time as musicians do, so he worked with music, both in training actors in his system of biomechanics and during rehearsals for productions, to cultivate a dance-like sense that would infuse the phrasing of everything on stage.

Lecoq's pedagogy includes working with music as a partner. Students work first with sound, followed by exercises where they are invited to respond through movement to the internal movements in pieces from the classical and jazz repertoires. Through embodying the music they find 'when it draws together, when it spirals, explodes, drops away, etc.'[283] The push/pull principle is rediscovered in learning to play *with* the music in this way. The work on musical graphs suggested in Section 5 has some affinity with this.

Directors Scott Graham and Steve Hoggett of Frantic Assembly use music – mostly instrumental tracks from their favourite artists – to set up a

'We embody it to understand it.'[284]

Jacques Lecoq

rehearsal environment, both as inspiration and to give a structure to sessions, so music informs the creation of the choreography. At times they allow music to lead the movement, so when rehearsing Mark Ravenhill's *pool (no water)*, for example, they asked actors to 'pay particular attention to the amount of silence and stillness throughout [an Imogen Heap] track', and to reference that same quality in a scene where the characters went to visit a hospitalised friend: 'The result was a scene of very precise choreography that was as much about not moving – a reflection of the song which often reduces itself to barely a breath.'[285] At other times they instruct actors to work against the music, and recount a turning point in rehearsals for *Hymns* when the CD player ran on beyond the track they were working to, and a quieter more reflective one came on: a new tempo and mood informed the quality of the work and they 'totally rediscovered the scene'.[286] Their discovery of how DJs structure club dance music by varying the BPM rates 'was like a newfound science to us, instantly understandable as one that centred round the focus and capacity of a crowd/audience to be moved'.[287] The way a DJ maps out the tempo, carrying the audience along initially at a steady rate, then increasing and decreasing the BPM to create intense peaks, followed by troughs for 'recovery' and respite, informs their approach to structuring the rhythmic through line of scenes. They have been known to time scenes to fit the length of the average pop music track of 3.5 minutes.

Music *'makes us aware of motion and space, and takes us more into the unconscious world when it is coupled with the text.'*[288]

Steven Berkoff

For Berkoff, music provides 'infinite inspiration, making us aware of moods sometimes in opposition to the text, sometimes provoking new thoughts, often creating the thought in the first place'.[289] He seldom uses canned music, more frequently working with a composer during rehearsals, whose improvisations stimulate ideas for movement. In Berkoff's productions, the imaginative world frequently incorporates live music, from the honky-tonk piano and nostalgic songs of *East* to the insistent drum at the start of *Coriolanus*. The acting ensemble who remained on stage throughout his production of *Hamlet* were dressed like orchestral musicians in dinner suits and black frocks, and, like an orchestra, they were physically creating sounds during the action. These not only created the atmosphere, such as the wind whistling round the turrets of Elsinore, but also worked on the psyche of the characters: when Ophelia arrived in mental disarray at the opening of Act Four, Scene Five, the chorus sang along to encourage her, 'just as wickedly insensitive people spur on a nutty person to wild, coarse and abandoned acts'.[290]

Music can be the key to creating mood, but also to manipulating an audience. Music has the power to induce a range of emotions. We unconsciously associate music with feeling; advertising and film exploit this relationship with an omnipresent underscore. Yet the right music can add structure as well as intensify emotional engagement. A film score is designed to mark and define transitions as well as pulling on heart strings or pumping up heartbeats. Film is a major influence on Frantic Assembly, evident in the soundtracks accompanying their shows. Although music does not always lead movement in rehearsals, the eventual soundtrack is designed to tally with the story and character journeys: 'a consistent sound [to] create an arc, in the same way as one might consider the arc of a storyline'.[291] Here music supports the emotional through line cinematically, an underscore serving a dramatic purpose in tandem and harmony with their directorial view. In *Peepshow*, for example, one particular song became associated with a couple, fully orchestrated in the beginning and eventually becoming a strings-only version as their relationship unravelled.

The opposite was precisely Brecht's aim; for him music was a tool to keep an audience on their toes. Remarkable music and songs, startlingly original in composition and style of presentation, punctuated his productions. Instead of sweeping an audience away on a wave of sentiment, the songs brought them back to earth with a jolt. Brecht referred to them as 'insertions', an indication of a shift to a different artistic level, since they are not designed to spring out of the actions within a play. He worked collaboratively with musicians, sometimes creating a melody and then forging an active relationship with a composer to create a sound palette integral to the tone of the production. Paul Dessau's sly and sardonic scoring for *Mother Courage*, using harmonica, muted trumpet and drum, is an example of such collaboration, with a mere four musicians – placed at the side of the stage as in oriental theatre – playing the trumpet for a fanfare or drum when necessary in addition to accompanying the songs. Brecht commented: 'Paul Dessau's music... is not meant to be particularly easy; like the stage set, it left something to be supplied by the audience.'[292]

As a shaping device, music is both mood-maker and mood-breaker. With live music, instruments attain a human quality when they are used to 'follow' the actors in accompaniment, creating a dialogue with performers. Those instruments don't need to be professionally played; they can be simple percussion and voice or vocal sound created by actors. Music by Richard Peaslee for Brook's production of *A Midsummer Night's Dream* used a variety of unconventional instruments, including bongo drums and tubular bells, with sound effects created with washboards and metal sheets, which could be played by actors in the ensemble. Despite an avowed aversion to 'theatre music', Sarah Kane deployed rain sticks in her production of *Woyzeck* at the Gate Theatre, with actors increasing and decreasing the volume of sound, helping to shape the overall momentum of the production.

Used to punctuate action or underscore it, to support it or interrupt it, even the simplest music has the power to redouble the intensity of experience in performance, creating a space in which we seem to exist in the 'now'. In addition to the slapstick and clowning of Kaos Theatre's wildly subversive *The Importance of Being Earnest*, the action was underscored by a mix of a hipster soundtrack and a capella versions of opera, performed with appropriate gusto by the acting ensemble. The choice of music may also connect to the setting or resetting of a play's political context. In the DonAd company's version of *Antigone*, Gaelic singing was accompanied by bourhans (Irish drums), their sound resonating with the memory of the dustbins banged in Belfast to alert the community to the presence of British soldiers.

When music is designated in a play, it is advisable to incorporate it into the rehearsal process rather than add it on as a technical side dish. And while music may not suit every play, used in rehearsal it has the virtue of attuning players to the topography of a scene and its emotional climate.

'Dynamic structure organises the play of the situation and the passions just as it organises the play of the body in movement.'[293]

Jacques Lecoq

Seeing a play as a series of tensions, constantly shifting and mutating like the dynamics in music, focuses attention on configuring and reconfiguring energy levels on stage. Energies surge and ebb in wave-like rhythms rather than in regular pulsing beats. Shifts in energy occur as a scene moves forward between units, and paying attention to these transitions gives shape and vitality to the pattern of dynamics operating beneath the surface action and dialogue. The preparatory work conducted on the dynamics of scenes in Section 5 now reaps benefits as those musical graphs, scene-scapes and soundscapes sowed the seeds for a shared feel for the undercurrents shaping dramatic action. That experiential sense of rhythmic flow can be applied to the whole play.

As you run more and more of the play together, an awareness of its orchestration is revealed and this is paramount in involving audience in the action. The French director Jean Luis Barrault draws attention to the compositional nature of theatre: 'the dramatic action of a play is brought out more by the rhythm of its orchestration than by psychological points.'[294] Rhythm has less to do with variations in speed and more to do with the way the action and delivery are accentuated; just as words can be stressed to provide emphasis, so too can moments of action.

Action is any change on stage, however small, which overtly or covertly affects those watching, and generates a moment of understanding, a moment of empathy or invokes their

'Involve the audience in the action of [the] play, make them feel part of it.'[295]

Joan Littlewood

kinaesthetic sense. Moments of stillness and silence are actions that resonate with potential meaning, just as turns and glances, or, at the high-voltage end of the spectrum, acrobatic moves. The meaning of an action is transmitted in the relationship between the levels of tension, the rhythm and the timing of execution.

Tension states

Stanislavsky was consummately skilled in illustrating how rhythms of the body affect behaviour and attract interest from spectators. He would demonstrate a line of physical actions in a variety of different rhythms, each relating to different circumstances, for example: buying a newspaper as if killing time while waiting for a train; buying one as the announcer signals the train's imminent departure; then buying one as the train actually starts. He executed the same line of physical actions in each improvisation, but performed each in a completely different rhythm. In this instance, he was performing according to the degree of urgency, showing how to manipulate the audience's attention by drawing them in through varying levels of tension in the body. There is an apparent similarity between this and the rehearsal tool known as the 'Seven Levels of Tension', which offer a kind of shorthand for degrees of intensity in engagement, from virtual inertia to the heightened terror of 'a bomb in the room that's about to detonate'. They are derived from Lecoq's pedagogy, as listed in the table below. John Wright's terms for these tension states sit alongside Lecoq's, although Wright views them as a cycle rather than a list, presenting them in a circular diagram moving from 'Exhausted' through to a level of tension so extreme that it is completely rigid.[296]

Lecoq	Wright
1. Catatonic	1. Exhausted
2. Relaxed	2. Laid-back
3. Neutral	3. One moment at a time
4. Alert	4. Neutral
5. Suspense	5. Is there a bomb?
6. Passionate	6. There is a bomb!
7. Tragic	7. The bomb is about to go off!
	8. Rigor mortis

Training with levels of tension opens up players to be more inventive, less clichéd. They are explored in the following sequence of exercises for those not already acquainted with them.

States of tension

Explore both ends of the spectrum initially to establish the outer extremes.

Working in pairs, start with Level 1, catatonic/exhausted: take turns to release all the tension in your body – which will mean lying down – while your partner checks to see that there is absolutely no tension left. This may mean they lift a leg or arm and gently shaking it before letting it back down to the floor. Let your partner take the weight of any limb or your head when they lift it slightly as this encourages you to let go of any remaining tension.

How does being completely relaxed make you feel?

Attempting to sit becomes a battle with gravity, with gravity having the upper hand. If you try to stand it is as though your body is burdened with lead. Walking involves enormous effort in dragging one foot past the other.

Then try the opposite extreme for Level 7, where tightening every muscle and sinew makes your whole body rigid. This can't be held for more than a few seconds if you do it properly. Partners can check to see outward evidence of tightened muscles in the neck and jaw area, and also verify that the knees are also tightly braced.

How does making every muscle tense make you feel?

To explore the scale between these two extremes, begin by walking in the space injecting tension into your body by degrees individually until you have a clear sense of each level in between.

Then return to pair work and experiment with the levels, playing around to see what happens when you vary them in a partnership.

What happens when players are interacting at the same level?

What happens when each player uses a different level?

Tension states can be applied to character work and interactions. At Level 1 the body is just surviving and speech verges on incoherent. The Ghost in *Hamlet* might be served through exploring 'exhausted', while Hamlet himself operates at Level 5 during their encounter, creating an instant contrast in how those two characters inhabit the stage. Level 2 is described by Lecoq as 'the body on holiday', an open and relaxed state. There is no relaxation by Level 4, which he states relates to 'realistic theatre, sensitive to situation', whereas the decisiveness necessary for action in situations occurs at Level 5. Passion informs Level 6, which becomes stylised in its use of playful anger. And Level 7 can only be simulated; Lecoq suggests it is similar to Noh theatre where movement is achieved through working with and against resistance.[297]

'The tension states is a very simple ideam which is why they're so useful.'[298]

John Wright

Tension states have no inherent meaning, although tension in the body is related to emotions. Meaning arises from the context. Any theatre text contains within it a level of bodily tension necessary to play it. Wright advocates clashing the tension state with an action, suggesting that running for a bus in 'exhausted' will be more interesting to watch than getting out of bed in 'exhausted', where the tension state more closely matches the action. Brecht wrote of how the actress playing Kattrin 'showed increasing exhaustion while drumming' in the scene where the dumb girl on the roof drums to save the village, as the peasant below tried to drown her out by chopping wood.[299]

The more players work with levels of tension the more they are able to capture the rhythm of each state. This is closely related to breathing. States of tension become internalised unconsciously in everyday living. Monitor your own breathing and you may find you recognise when more agitated states are evident in shorter breaths and relaxed states rely on deeper and longer breaths. In our daily lives we are more familiar with the lower range of tensions states, from Levels 1 to 4, and those levels of physical intensity are more dominant in plays demanding a lifelike degree of psychological realism. Exploring the upper range offers the possibility of playing levels of intensity with a degree of lightness that does not compromise the seriousness of more dramatic or tragic situations.

Tension states offer an emotional vocabulary that can be imported to inform relationships between characters as players experiment with different ranges. An ability to switch between levels at a detailed level in exchanges of dialogue promotes a focused attention on the present moment. Identifying – and playing – different tension states can prevent actors falling into each other's rhythm, particularly in scenes between two characters in a sustained argument, such as the final act of *Top Girls*.

'In life, we tend to internalise our states of tension and change [them via] the breath.'[300]

John Wright

Revisiting character work to re-evaluate and modify players' initial choices is necessary in the latter stages of rehearsals. Sometimes players may not have relinquished their own personal and habitual inner pulse, but adopting a different energy level can help the character come alive. Recalibrating tension states in the light of the earlier work on the character journeys becomes vital when playing through the whole play. A useful analogy is to imagine a character's pulse rate – asking what level of anxiety operates in them at specific points in the play, for example, which is similar to using percentages.

The level of anxiety will be influenced by points when events occur in relation to the complete journey in some cases, particularly with characters for whom the stakes rise incrementally during the play. At this point in rehearsals, attending to these levels accentuates a sense of the different facets presented by a character. Even in a play as minimalist as *Waiting for Godot*, where there is no apparent change in circumstance by the end of the play, there are moments of pressure that demonstrate the essential nature of Valdimir and Estragon, and their varying degrees of acceptance in their situation; playing with tension states serves to differentiate these.

Using runs, whether of complete sections, of several scenes together, of acts, is hugely beneficial. Although repetition is the main focus during these later stages of rehearsals, it is not necessarily the enemy of inspiration, quite often the reverse. Moments within a scene that seemed highly effective during earlier rehearsals can often lose their potency when played as part of a longer episode or sequence. When something isn't working it is rarely the fault of an individual person but of the choices made in rehearsal. At this stage, where you are dealing with the 'bigger picture', decisions made previously at the level of smaller details begin to announce an impact on the whole. Look out for points where tension states need adjustment, some variation in the rhythm of an episode is required or injections of pace are needed, as well as points where the energy choices players are making for characters are either too blatant or too minimalist, so they can be modified accordingly. Editing becomes necessary: eliminating what no longer seems to be working, usually when the first flush of excitement at a particular discovery has faded; pruning any excess that might smack of indulgence; perhaps also elaborating on ideas that have not yet reached their potential. And, especially with highly physical or precise choreography, it is necessary to 'mark through' for accuracy in placement and timing.

'Tempo is particular to the story being told.'[301]

Steve Waters

The most important thing to bear in mind is the audience's journey through the whole play; this has to be the primary factor governing new decisions. It is about managing the expectations of spectators – building tension or dropping it, privileging moments where time seems to stop.

Principles of playfulness still apply during these final stages. Playing with pace and tempo can keep the work alive, injecting freshness into running scenes and sequences.

Pacing

'Runs should dominate the final period of rehearsal.'[302]

Mike Alfreds

The earlier you use full runs, the more actors become adjusted to the flow of a play. And everyone needs to be aware of the composition of the play in its entirety to be an effective component in its performance. Those early workshops in mapping the play and charting the character journeys should ensure everyone has a strong purchase on the story being told.

There is a connection between the speed at which events occur and the kind of play. Comedy usually plays faster than tragedy. But there is danger in presuming a faster pace suits only comedy. Ponderousness can cause serious drama to drag. Brecht advocated a quality of *ease* in performance for every play, regardless of the perceived genre, and the actual German word he used is *leichtigkeit*, which means lightness as well as ease, an ambiguity the translator of his work John Willett, suggests is 'impossible to convey in one English word'.[303] Such lightness in playing is what Ayckbourn found in rehearsals for *A View from the Bridge* referred to earlier, and consequently it ran much shorter than previous productions.

'There is something naturally light and easy about the theatre.'[304]

Bertolt Brecht

Playing sections first in slow motion and then like a speeded-up replay reveals points where pace and tempo can be modified; this has the benefit of giving players a renewed sense of fun that can transfer into lightness and ease. A speed run, i.e. running the scene or play at the speed of thought rather than how fast you can speak, invariably identifies problems and occasionally offers solutions. Once a degree of speed is achieved, things that may not have previously worked can sometimes fall into place, as though speed injects a different energy which inspires solutions. This is frequently related to entrances and exits. The *Route map* exercise in Section 3 and the *Greetings* exercise at the end of Section 4 flagged up the inherent dynamic in every entrance and exit as key to the overall performance continuum. Once at the stage of running the whole play, their significance as active agents in modifying pace and tempo becomes more apparent. Paying attention to these in terms of players' energy reveals where the pace sags. Making sure players bring energy on with them and leave energy on stage when they go as has a beneficial effect on the fluidity of the performance.

Macbeth, admittedly the shortest of Shakespeare's output, can be electrifying played straight through according to David Edgar, since urgency is matched with urgency for most of the play. Calendar time in the play is probably around six months, yet for much of it time feels quite frenetic and any moments of apparent stability, such as the banquet scene, are soon disrupted by action that creates more intensity. When incident piles on incident it can be counterproductive to insist on an interval. It is worth noting that there were no intervals in theatre until around 1609, when theatre moved indoors and the plays were forced to stop for a short time for the candles to be trimmed. Deciding where to place one is not always automatic. At the front of the 1985 edition of *Top Girls*, Caryl Churchill states the play was originally written in three acts and she still finds that structure clearer: 'Act One, the dinner; Act Two, Angie's story; Act Three, the year before. But now intervals do hold things up, so in the original production we made it two acts with the interval after what is here Act Two, Scene Two. Do whichever you prefer.'

The pattern of *Hamlet* is halting, as Shakespeare plays with time and tension like wires being stretched and pulled in different directions. In Gregory Doran's 2009 production for the RSC, the interval was placed in the middle of Act Three, Scene Three, creating a pause in Hamlet's speech as he comes upon Claudius praying alone and has the opportunity to kill him. For those seeing the play for the first time they might believe that Hamlet is actually going to succeed in avenging

'It is about creating these little moments where the audience doubt that they know it.'[305]

David Tennant

his father's death; for those familiar with *Hamlet* the choice was a bold and radical one. In both cases, the audience returned to their seats with renewed zest and interest.

Very busy scenes often need less speed to avoid becoming muddied and allow key moments to be absorbed. More static scenes can often take quick delivery of dialogue since the audience focuses more on listening than watching. And scenes affect one another by virtue of their placement in relation to each other. In plays with multiple short scenes in different locations, such as *Woyzeck*, you need to discover contrasts in tempo. The swifter the text moves when predominantly in one location, as in a play like *A View from the Bridge*, the more distinct the transitions need to be between one segment and the next. A premium pace is not reliant on the pace of movement or words but the pace of the flow of information to the audience.

'If the story's unclear, the play will seem longer.'[306]

Simon Callow

Opening scenes are important for many reasons, not least in setting up expectations, but also in relation to pace. Their purpose may be to settle the audience into a state where they accept whatever you throw at them afterwards, and in this sense they are the equivalent of a 'departure lounge' – a bridge between the everyday world and world of play. Yet playing the first scene of a play as though it is merely a transition to the rest of the play can be misguided. First scenes need to be given a weight of their own. This means playing them as though the outcome might be different. The lights come up on an empty hotel room at the start of *Blasted* so the audience absorb the setting first. The opening is quiet and measured, slow in pace from the entrance of Cate, who stands gazing at everything in the room, the audience lulled into close observation of her wide-eyed awe, trying to figure out the nature of the relationship between this naive young woman and her uncouth partner. This almost gentle, relaxed introduction to the play is soon disfigured as events unfold so it cannot be rushed, otherwise it will seem too prescient; the pace forces the audience to pay attention to details and adds to the surprise in what happens next.

Shakespeare thrusts the audience into the nervy atmosphere of soldiers on the battlements at night in *Hamlet*. War is expected. It's a scared place. We are immediately in the land of a thriller. The opening line 'Who's there?' catapults us into the tension. Within thirty lines the Ghost appears. The anxiety transmits to the audience so there is no gentle relaxed introduction here. Instead we are locked on via the suspense of what might happen next.

Mother Courage looked back as the cart rumbled onto the stage at the opening of Brecht's play, one backward glance to indicate the cart had come a long way. And he tells how, in the revised production, Helene Weigel, playing Courage, suggested replacing the lusty, overtly dramatic style of singing of the original with the idea that it be sung 'as a realistic business song [that] pictured the long journey to the war'.[307] This added to the effect of the backward glance, putting the audience in a state of reflection on war rather than on the prospect of an evening's entertainment.

Quite the reverse happens with a Frantic show. Frantic Assembly have developed the idea of what they call the 'pre-show', laying claim to the theatre space and the audience's attention. They gauge a moment when about fifty per cent of the audience are in their seats to unleash pulsating music and, sometimes, a movement sequence onstage, that sets the tone for the performance to come. This exploits the idea of theatre as 'event', so that the play has already started in a sense before the lights actually go down. They often set the sound at a level that forces the audience to raise their voices to converse with each other, thereby raising the energy in the 'room' and increasing the audience's sense of expectation. The pre-show is: 'a precious device... as invaluable and essential part of what we perceive to be the theatrical experience [which] creates a sense of event by asking the audience to commit to the experience just that little bit earlier than they might usually expect, to give us just that little bit more.'[308] This comment recognises the importance of the audience for performers, a point echoed in Dame Judi Dench's revelation that she has the audience pre-show hum piped from the auditorium into her dressing room before being called to the stage.

Transitions between scenes and acts are significant part of the audience experience. Often it is only when you get to the stage of running the whole play that decisions about dealing with these arise. Blackouts can make spectators feel cut off. If it is not necessary to cut the light then don't, though if you do need darkness it is worth considering whether sound can add anything. Sound is an effective 'cover' for scene changes, used either as a tension-breaker or to maintain the tension level. Directing the first production of *Blasted*, James Macdonald came up with the idea of using the sound of rain between scenes 'to get from A to B to C and cover us running around in the dark'.[310] The sound was engineered too so that rain got harder and harder until it comes through the roof in the final scene. Kane liked the idea so much that it was incorporated into later editions of the text.

'There is a frequency that you tune in to and it is literally in the air, a channel between the audience and you.'[309]

Michael Sheen

There is a rhythm to be found in moving from scene to scene, whether you treat the transitions as interruptions or find ways to weave them seamlessly into the flow or, as in the case cited of *Blasted*, fit them into the image structure of the play. Robert Lepage points to the fact that we live 'in a language of jump-cuts and sound bites; and if you're not going to use that as a storyteller in the theatre, they're at the end of the story before you are.'[311] Film offers a vocabulary in its editing terminology: cuts, fades, dissolves, cross-fades and wipes are familiar terms which describe the links between images. The way actors for the next scene enter as the previous scene comes to an end in has become a modern convention that replicates the use of the 'dissolve' or 'cross-fade' in films and adds to the fluidity of performance. Quick cuts are virtually written into Miller's *A View from the Bridge*, but a similar effect can be created by the speed of switching from one unit to the next to create a sense of immediacy in the flow. Cross-fading allows the blending and blurring of action between locations, creating seamless transitions. In other cases, scene changes can be an opportunity to interrupt the flow or allow time for audiences to digest what has happened. Bond's *Saved* is a beautifully engineered play with narrative gaps between scenes;

changes executed with visible stage hands removing or reinstating furniture, as in the Lyric production of 2011, allow the audience time for reflection. In productions where an ensemble remains on stage it makes sense to use players to change any set. Using players-in-character to change scenes can be an effective way to segue from one to the next if you want to maintain the flow and atmosphere.

Durational actions in the script serve to dictate pace on occasion, with a concomitant effect on the audience. The kettle has to boil in the final scene of *Top Girls* and the dialogue has to fit with that technical demand, while the sound and sight of the kettle boiling triggers recognition in the reality of domestic life, and perhaps, arguments in our kitchens. When Harry visits Len like a ghost in Scene Twelve, the young man is packing his suitcase. Len continues packing and moves the suitcase along the bed, as though he is intending to leave, until Harry eventually says he'd like it if he stayed – and Len slides the suitcase under the bed. This penultimate scene is quietly measured, in contrast to the heated exchanges between everyone in the previous one when tempers boiled over, and it is only now that Harry articulates his perspective on his marriage and life. It puts the audience in reflective mood, one which continues into the final silent scene where 'life goes on' as Len mends the chair.

For performers, endings are also where the life of the play goes on, since it is only when rehearsals come to an end that the real business of unfurling a play in front of an audience starts. All the testing of possibilities in rehearsals now begins a new chapter, since each audience will animate players in a renewed search for a play's meaning. Theatre takes us out of ourselves in the sense that we go into a dreamworld where time seems suspended. We can be swept away on the tide of a well-told tale, what Brecht decried as its role as 'opiate for the people'. A play can also take us into ourselves, confronting us with both public and intensely private dilemmas: conflicts and concerns that lie deep within us, and provoke us to question not only ourselves, but our humanity and the humanity of others. When it does all of these at the same time it is truly remarkable. Whatever play you work on in whatever style, the ending is where the dramatist has their final say; it is the final image that an audience takes home with them. The importance of endings is neatly summed up by

Lecoq: 'it is the last act that counts, and one always remembers the ending better than the beginning. It manifests the quality of the whole.'[312] Bearing this in mind should fuel the process of creative interpretation of a play from the outset.

Afterword

The ideas and approaches in this book are intended to enrich the vocabulary of everyone involved in the choices and judgements made in the rehearsal room or studio workshop. A central ethic is to keep the eventual audience in mind, since they will share in the act of imagining the play. Using members of the company to watch when they're not performing has advantages in testing the effectiveness of ideas during the process, as well as replicating the way spectator attention can empower and energise players.

'The moment we feel that a third person is watching, the conditions of a rehearsal are transformed.'[313]

Peter Brook

The concept of the text as active relates to the active nature of spectatorship. As pointed out throughout this book, theatre in its purest form is a sharing between actors and audience. A kinaesthetic approach to preparing the performance of a play resonates with its eventual audience on multi-sensory levels. The long-held beliefs of theatre practitioners and scholars concerning the empathic responses of audiences to what unfolds on stage appear to be confirmed by the discovery of mirror neurons, which fire in the human brain in response to actions observed, and the idea of emotion as not only contagious but amplified in the presence of others is also gaining credence from studies in cognitive science.[314]

Play builds a capacity for intuitive and imaginative responses, as well as refining and sharpening physical reactions; as such it has a vital place in theatre-making. Building rapport between players is an essential element, whether devising a piece or working with texts. A common root lies in the use of improvisation and collaboration, a way of working that relies on mutual respect for everyone involved.

Whether the directors and performers quoted in the pages of this book have experience in devised theatre or not, they all recognise the value of collaborative working methods. And many reiterate the fact that

'It's always about collaboration and the really theatrical ideas coming right off the floor.'[315]

Nancy Meckler

being brave, resourceful and fearless in rehearsals is nurtured by fun, for seriousness in the content of a play is not undermined by working through playful means. Play cultivates improvisatory attitudes, and improvising the situations characters confront before tackling the words as written facilitates a deeper shared understanding.

The aim is to integrate the corporeal and the verbal, transforming the dramatist's ideas into embodied theatrical form to create spatial and visual impact. Making the utmost of the language of the body and relationships in space between players is crucial to creating powerful effects on viewers. Framing and placement are vital tools in the transmission of meaning that goes beyond reproducing everyday life.

'Try the scene every which way, constantly looking for different ways, different choices.'[316]

Katie Mitchell

While round-the-table discussion of the text is relegated to a back seat in this book, it does not mean that analysis is ignored. Analysis comes through experiential and kinaesthetic engagement with the structure of the whole and its constituent parts; enacting and embodying the thoughts and feelings of characters comes through engaging with their situations. And is it is worth noting that cognitive science has also begun dismantling the prevalence of Cartesian mind/body dualism, since observations of chemical activity in our neural networks confirm interactivity between muscles and mind, the kind of integration that undergirds the concept of embodiment. Movement and gesture are as expressive and eloquent as words spoken, image structures as important as clarity of narrative. Studying a play should always be an active process.

Rehearsal is a pragmatic and empirical process: physical and spatial investigations work alongside the cognitive: the test is 'does it work?' The word rehearsal has differing defini-

> '*The word rehearsal literally means "to rake over" – preparing the ground.*'[317]
>
> Simon McBurney

tions in different languages: *probing* in German for example. The derivation of the word rehearsal actually lies with an old French word *rehercier*, a term for the second phase of ploughing when the soil is sifted and stirred to prepare it for sowing, which implies a highly active approach. In English it implies 'listening' when we think of it as re-hear-sal, although this book advocates what Frantic Assembly call 'physical listening' as well as the auditory kind.

Applying this within devising methodologies to rehearsals for scripted plays is an invaluable route to discovering that texts are inherently active. It can perhaps revive a regard for the metaphorical nature of theatre, distinguishing it from mediated forms and inspiring future practices. When metaphors are rich enough, as they are in the historical and modern classical repertoire, the sense of theatre as an imaginative game of make-believe continues to entrance. Classic plays are also great performance gymnasiums, offering players an 'acting workout' that is a valuable constituent of training. Above all, they are great stories, and, as humans, we are hard-wired for a love of storytelling.

Select Bibliography

Aciman, Alexander and Rensin, Emmett *Twitterature, the World's Greatest Books Retold Through Twitter.* London: Penguin, 2009

Alexander, Catherine *Complicite, Teachers' Notes – Devising*, 2001. PDF available from www.complicite.org.uk

Alfreds, Mike *Different Every Night.* London: Nick Hern Books, 2001

Ayckbourn, Alan *The Crafty Art of Playmaking.* London: Faber, 2002

Barba, Eugenio *On Directing and Dramaturgy: Burning the House.* London: Routledge, 2010

Barba, Eugenio and Savarese, Nicole *A Dictionary of Theatre Anthroplogy: The Secret Art of the Performer*, edited and compiled by Richard Gough, translated by Robert Fowler. London: Routledge, 1991

Barrault, Jean-Louis *Memories for Tomorrow: The Memoirs of Jean-Louis Barrault*, trans. by Jonathan Griffin. London: Thames and Hudson, 1974

Berkoff, Steven *I am Hamlet.* London: Faber, 1989

— *Meditations on Metamorphosis.* London: Faber, 1995

— 'Three Theatre Manifestos' in Gambit, Vol.8 No.32, 1978

Berry, Cicely *From Word to Play: A Handbook for Directors.* London: Oberon Books, 2008

— *Text in Action*. London: Virgin Books, 2001

Berry, Ralph *On Directing Shakespeare: Interviews with Contemporary Directors*. London: Hamish Hamilton, 1989

Bigsby, Christopher (Ed.) *The Cambridge Companion to Arthur Miller*. Cambridge: CUP, 1997

Bogart, Anne *A Director Prepares: Seven Eessays on Art and Theatre*. London & New York, 2001

Bradby, David *Beckett: Waiting for Godot*. Cambridge: CUP, 2001

Brook, Peter *There Are No Secrets: Thoughts on Acting and Theatre*. London: Methuen, 1993

— *Threads of Time: A Memoir*. London: Methuen, 1998

Complicite *Rehearsal Notes*, coordinated by Hannah Schultz. London: Complicite, 2010

Davis, Rib *Writing Dialogue for Scripts*. London: A&C Black, 1998

Donnellan, Declan *The Actor and the Target*. London: Nick Hern Books, 2002

Dromgoole, Dominic *Performance Style and Gesture in Western Theatre*. London: Oberon Books, 2007

— *The Full Room: An A-Z of Contemporary Playwriting*. London: Methuen, 2000

Edgar, David *How Plays Work*. London: Nick Hern Books, 2009

Esslin, Martin *An Anatomy of Drama*. London: Sphere Books, 1978

Eyre, Richard *Talking Theatre: Interviews with Theatre People*. London: Nick Hern Books, 2009

Field, Syd *Screenplay: The Foundations of Screenwriting*, revised edition. New York: Bantam Dell, 2005

Fitzsimmons, Linda *File on Churchill*. London: Methuen, 1989

Freshwater, Helen 'Physical Theatre: Complicite and the Question of Authority' in *A Concise Companion to Contemporary British and Irish Drama*, edited by Nadine Holdsworth and Mary Luckhurst. Malden and Oxford: Blackwell Publishing, 2013

Gaskill, William *Words into Action: Finding the Life of the Play.* London: Nick Hern Books, 2010

— *A Sense of Direction: Life at the Royal Court.* London: Faber, 1988

Gabriella Giannachi and Mary Luckhurst (eds.) *On Directing: Interviews with Directors.* London: Faber and Faber, 1999

Gooch, Steve *Writing a Play*, third edition. London: A & C Black, 2001

Graham, Scott and Hoggett, Steven *The Frantic Assembly Book of Devising.* London: Routledge, 2010

Greig, Noel *Playwriting: A Practical Guide.* London: Routledge, 2005

Griffiths, Stuart *How Plays are Made.* London: Heinemann, 1982

Hall, Peter *Exposed by the Mask.* London: Oberon Books, 2000

Haynes, John & Knowlson, James *Images of Beckett.* Cambridge: CUP, 2003

Hodge, Alison (ed.) *Actor Training*, second edition. Abingdon: Routledge, 2010

Holdsworth, Nadine *Joan Littlewood.* London: Routledge, 2006

Hurley, Erin *Theatre and Feeling.* Basingstoke: Palgrave Macmillan, 2010

Iball, Helen *Sarah Kane's Blasted.* London: Continuum International, 2008

Knowlson, James and Elizabeth (eds.) *Beckett Remembering, Remembering Beckett: Uncollected Interviews with Samuel Beckett and Memories of Those Who Knew Him.* London: Bloomsbury, 2007

Kustow, Michael *Theatre@risk.* London: Methuen, 2000

Leach Robert *Theatre Workshop: Joan Littlewood and the Making of Modern British Theatre.* Exeter: Exeter University Press, 2006

Lecoq, Jacques (edited by David Bradby) *Theatre of Movement and Gesture.* Abingdon: Routledge, 2006

— *The Moving Body: Teaching Creative Theatre*. London: Methuen, 2000

Leipacher, Mark *Catching the Light: Sam Mendes and Simon Russell Beale*. London: Oberon Books, 2011

Little, Ruth *The Young Vic Book: Theatre Work and Play*. London: Methuen, 2004

Littlewood, Joan *Joan's Book*. London: Methuen, 1994

Luckhurst, Mary and Veltman, Chloe *On Acting: Interviews with Actors*. London: Faber and Faber: 2001

McAuley, Gay *Space in Performance: Making Meaning in the Theatre*. Ann Arbor: University of Michigan Press, 2000

Mamet, David *True and False: Heresy and Common Sense for the Actor*. London: Faber and Faber, 1998

— *A Whore's Profession* London: Faber and Faber, 1994

Manfull, Helen *Taking Stage: Women Directors on Directing*. London: Methuen, 1999

Marowitz, Charles, Milne, Tom and Hale, Owen (eds.) *The Encore Reader: A Chronicle of the New Drama*. London: Methuen & Co., 1965

Murray, Simon *Jacques Lecoq*. London: Routledge, 2003

Newlove, Jean *Laban for Actors and Dancers: Putting Laban's Theory into Practice – A Step-by-Step Guide*. London: Nick Hern Books, 1993

Reade, Simon *Cheek by Jowl: Ten Years of Celebration*. Bath: Absolute Classics, 1991

Saunders, Graham *Love me or kill me: Sarah Kane and the Theatre of Extremes*. Manchester: Manchester University Press, 2002

Shevtsova, Maria *Robert Wilson*. London: Routledge, 2007

Shevtsova, Maria and Innes, Christopher *Directors/Directing: Conversations on Theatre*. Cambridge University Press, 2009

Smiley, Sam *Playwriting: The Structure of Action*, revised edition. New Haven and London: Yale University Press, 2005

Toporkov, Vasily Osopovich *Stanislavski in Rehearsal: The Final Years*, trans. Christine Edwards. New York: Theatre Arts Books, 1979

Tushingham, David *Live 1. Food for the Soul: A New Generation of British Theatremakers*. London: Methuen, 1994

— *Live 2. Not What I Am: The Experience of Performing*. London: Methuen, 1995

Walter, Harriet *Other People's Shoes*. London: Nick Hern Books, 2003

Waters, Steven *The Secret Life of Plays*. London: Nick Hern Books, 2010

Wekworth, Manfred *Daring to Play: A Brecht Companion*, edited by Anthony Hozier, trans. by Rebecca Braun. London: Routledge, 2011

Wright, John *Why is That So Funny?: A Practical Exploration of Physical Comedy*. London: Nick Hern Books, 2006

Plays

Beckett, Samuel *Waiting for Godot*, 2nd edition. London: Faber and Faber, 1965

Berkoff, Steven *Greek* in *The Collected Plays Volume 1*. London: Faber and Faber, 1994

Bond, Edward *Saved*. London: Methuen Drama, 2011

Brecht, Bertolt *Mother Courage and Her Children*, trans. John Willett. London: Eyre Methuen Ltd., 1980

Büchner, Georg *Woyzeck*, trans. Gregory Motton. London: Nick Hern Books, 1996

Churchill, Caryl *Top Girls*. London: Methuen Drama, 1991

— *Blue Heart*. London: Nick Hern Books, 1997

Kane, Sarah *Blasted* in *Complete Plays*. London: Methuen, 2001

Miller, Arthur *A View from the Bridge*. Penguin Classics edition, 2009

Shakespeare, William *Hamlet, Macbeth, A Midsummer Night's Dream*

Sophocles *Antigone*, trans. and introduced by Marianne McDonald. London: Nick Hern Books, 2000

Wilde, Oscar *The Importance of Being Earnest,* introduced by Dan Rebellato. London: Nick Hern Books, 1995

Endnotes

Foreword

1. See Lecoq, Jacques (2000) *The Moving Body*, New York: Theatre Arts Books (Routledge), p. 169. *Tout bouge* was also the title of Lecoq's own lecture-demonstration, which he performed all over the world.

2. McCaw, Dick (2001) Foreword to *Through the Body: A Practical Guide to Physical Theatre*, Dymphna Callery. London: Nick Hern Books

3. Yarrow, Ralph and Franc Chamberlain (2002) *Jacques Lecoq and the British Theatre*, London and New York: Routledge, p. 27.

Introduction

4. There is a select bibliography which includes sources which have informed the book, and suggestions for further reading.

5. Declan Donnellan in GIANNACHI & LUCKHURST, 1999:19

6. DAVIS, 1998:1

7. ALFREDS, 2007:120

8. BARBA, 2010:9

9. *Ibid.*:10

10. HARROP, 1992:77

11. ALFREDS, 2007:180

12. Although Vsevelod Meyerhold, Jacques Copeau, Edward Gordon Craig and Bertolt Brecht swept away the proscenium arch in European theatres and pioneered the concept of the stage as an empty space, where levels and light threw the physicality of actors into relief during the early years of the twentieth century, it was Littlewood's productions, designed and lit by John Bury, that the idea of an uncluttered stage arrived in Britain in the 1950s.

13. Annabel Arden in LUCKHURST & VELTMAN, 2001:3

14. AYCKBOURN, 2002:138

15. GRAHAM & HOGGETT, 2009:29

16. ALFREDS, 2007:352

17. Increasing numbers of movement directors working on high-profile productions in British theatre at the beginning of the new millennium have trained with Lecoq, notably Toby Sedgewick, whose work on the National Theatre's *War Horse* (2009) and *Frankenstein* (2010), and the Opening Ceremony of the Olympic Games in London (2012) has earned critical accolades; Jane Gibson, who has worked closely with Cheek by Jowl; Joseph Alford, who is artistic director of his own company Theatre O, but also a movement director for Katie Mitchell; and it is worth noting that David Sabal, the person responsible for creating the National Theatre's live streaming in cinemas, is also a Lecoq graduate. Several significant practitioners in contemporary theatre, including Steven Berkoff, Ariane Mnouchkine and Simon McBurney also trained at Lecoq's school; Robert Lepage attended Quebec City Conservatory where he was taught by teachers using Lecoq's philosophy and pedagogical approach.

18. Simon McBurney in GIANNACHI & LUCKHURST, 1999:70

19. Until 2013 Graham and Hoggett were co-directors; since then Scott Graham has taken over as sole Artistic Director of the company.

20. WALTER, 2003:60

21. 'A Goodbye Note from Joan' in MAROVITZ, et al,1965:133

22. LITTLEWOOD, 1994:199

23. I am only too aware of the preponderance of Caucasian males in the selection of playwrights. However, syllabi are slow to change, and, to quote Spinoza: 'if you want the present to be different from the past, study the past.' I use cross-gender and cross-racial casting when exploring a play in workshops, which often throws up interesting and valid discussions about the nature of the 'canon' and the preponderance of gendered perspectives that can fuel and inform critical analysis.

Section 1: Plays and Audiences

24. Mark Rylance interviewed by Mark Lawson, BBC2, June 2013

25. HARROP, 1992:108

26. Simon McBurney in SHEVTSOVA & INNES, 2009:167

27.   Declan Donnellan in BERRY, 1989:202

28.   Robert Lepage in conversation with Richard Eyre, *Platform Papers 3: Directors*, Royal National Theatre, 1992:28

29.   WEKWERTH, 2011:57

30.   WATERS, 2010:166

31.   GRAHAM & HOGGETT, 2009:131

32.   EDGAR, 2009:65

33.   LECOQ, 2006:78

34.   WRIGHT, 2006:xvi

35.   AYCKBOURN, 2002:3

36.   WRIGHT, 2006:11 and 21

37.   Sam Mendes in LEIPACHER, 2011:43

38.   Caryl Churchill in FITZSIMMONS, 1989:86 and 62

39.   Glenda Jackson in MAROWITZ, 1986:156

40.   'We would not advise new companies to take the risks we took with the John Osborne Estate... We arrogantly abused the text, no matter how noble we thought our intentions were.' Graham and Hoggett, http://www.franticassembly.co.uk/media/media/downloads/Frantic _Assembly_Resource_Pack.pdf p. 4 Accessed 11/01/12

41.   GRAHAM & HOGGETT, 2009:171

42.   WRIGHT, 2006:5

43.   Büchner wrote the play in 1836 but it was not performed until 1913, directed by Reinhardt in Munich.

44.   Maria Shevtsova's illuminating book on Robert Wilson gives a detailed description of the production and Wilson's use of every theatrical element. Shevtsova, Maria, *Robert Wilson*. London: Routledge, 2007

45.   Howard Brenton interviewed by Laura Silverman, *The Times: Playlist* July 17–23, 2010:18

46.   GREIG, 2005:46

47.   *New Statesman*, 1982, quoted in: Churchill, Caryl, *Top Girls with commentary and notes by Bill Naismith*, London Methuen 1991:xxxv

48.   Sarah Kane in Giammarco (1997) in SAUNDERS, 2009:98

49.   He heard the story of a longshoreman who betrayed his relatives when researching *The Hook: a play for the screen* (never produced) working with Elia Kazan, who went on to direct *On the Waterfront*.

Elia Kazan was one of those who did name names to the House Committee on Un-American Activities.

50. GREIG, 2005:27

51. Caryl Churchill is a playwright often mentioned in relation to collaboration with actors since her work with Joint Stock on *Cloud Nine* and *Fen*. She points out in an interview: 'The idea for a workshop isn't necessarily the idea for a play' when referring to the workshop on sexual politics that fuelled *Cloud Nine*. Peter Brook, Complicite, Kneehigh and Frantic Assembly all work with writers during the process of creating a devised piece and also on occasions when adapting extant texts.

52. David Mamet uses this phrase when writing about the need to resist narrating through dialogue in film (MAMET, 1994:390), but I find it serves as memorable pointer for student actors and directors to consider dialogue as the gloss on the action in theatre.

53. WRIGHT, 2006:63

54. LECOQ, 2002:22

55. GREIG, 2005:27

56. MAMET, 1994:118

57. EDGAR, 2009:99

58. MAMET, 1994:114

59. http://www.robinkelly.btinternet.co.uk/eaton.htm accessed 11/01/12

60. HALL, 2000:15

61. STEIN, 1935:111

62. Peter Brook in KALMAN, 1992:110

63. HALL, 2000:14

64. DROMGOOLE, 2007:290

65. CALLOW, 1985:219

66. BARBA, 2010:23

Section 2: Serious Play

67. CALLOW, 1985:179

68. Simon McBurney in EYRE, 2009:304

69. WRIGHT, 2006:65

70. Beckett's own oft-repeated comment about the play was that the characters are all engaged in playing games: 'Didi and Gogo are

players, ' he said. 'They play games, as do Pozzo and Lucky.' Beckett quoted in GUSSOW, 1996:3

71. AYCKBOURN, 2002:144

72. BROOK, 1998:149

73. *Ibid.*

74. Robert Lepage in conversation with Richard Eyre, *Platform Papers 3: Directors*, Royal National Theatre 1992:27

75. HARROP, 1992:57

76. Complicite Resource Pack for *The Chairs*, 1998

77. WRIGHT, 2006:80

78. GRAHAM & HOGGETT, 2009:130

79. LECOQ, 2006:109

80. WRIGHT, 2006:41; John Wright gives this in-depth coverage in his book *Why is that so Funny?: A Practical Exploration of Physical Comedy*, which, despite its title, has a multitude of games and exercises not all related specifically to comedy.

81. LECOQ, 2006:77

82. WRIGHT, 2006:16

83. *Ibid.*:35–36

84. *Ibid.*:88

85. HARROP, 1992:23

86. LITTLE, 2004:201

87. BROOK, 1998:85

88. *Ibid.*:150

89. LECOQ, 2002:93

90. *Ibid.*:92

91. LECOQ, 2006:4

92. LECOQ, 2000:104

93. DROMGOOLE, 2007:286

94. LECOQ, 2006:78

95. LECOQ, 2000:46–7

96. LECOQ, 2002:22

97. LECOQ, 2006:4

98. BOGART, 2001:105

99. WALTER, 2003:94

Section 3: Mapping a Play

100. Emma Rice, *The Essay, On Directing*, BBC Radio 3, 14/02/12

101. Annabel Arden in MANFULL, 1999:120

102. Sam Mendes in LEIPACHER, 2011:21

103. ALEXANDER, Complicite *Teachers Notes – Devising*, 2001

104. David Lan in LITTLE, 2004:202

105. Holmberg, 1996:202, quoted by SHEVTSOVA, 2007:54

106. READE, 1991:65. Simon Reade is referring here to Cheek by Jowl and how the environment is a major factor in their productions.

107. WATERS, 2010:58

108. BERKOFF, 1989:4

109. *Ibid.*:3

110. BERKOFF, 1978:8

111. ALEXANDER, Complicite *Teachers Notes – Devising*, 2001

112. CALLOW, 1985:156

113. ALEXANDER, Complicite *Teachers Notes – Devising*, 2001

114. COMPLICITE, 2010:99

115. This sequences of exercise appears in the Complicite *Teachers Notes – Devising*, 2001

116. LECOQ, 2000:95

117. Paul Hunter from www.digitaltheatre.com/production/details/the-comedy-of-errors/Directing Comedy of Errors, 2010

118. ACIMAN & RENSIN, 2009:10

119. LUCKHURST & VELTMAN, 2001:28

120. Emma Rice, *The Essay, On Directing*, BBC Radio 3, 14/02/12

121. *Ibid.*

122. Annie Castledine in MANFULL, 1999:87

123. Declan Donnellan in GIANNACHI & LUCKHURST, 1999:20

124. COMPLICITE, *Rehearsal Notes*, 2011:75

125. Jane Hartley, unpublished interview with the author, 4/07/11

126. Nancy Meckler in MANFULL, 1999:70

Section 4: Charting Journeys

127.　WATERS, 2010:97

128.　Ariane Mnouchkine in LECOQ, 2006:135

129.　HARROP, 1992:21

130.　WALTER, 2003:37

131.　Abigail Rokison interview (2009): David Tennant on Hamlet, Shakespeare, 5:3, 292-304, DOI:10.1080/17450910903138062, date accessed 14/07/2013

132.　David Lan in LITTLE, 2004:212

133.　CALLOW, 1985:212

134.　GREIG, 2005:84

135.　AYCKBOURN, 2002:35–36

136.　Jane Hartley, unpublished interview with the author, 4/07/11

137.　CALLOW, 1985:61

138.　BRECHT 1980:117

139.　MAMET, 1998:84

140.　WALTER, 2003:76

141.　BRECHT, 1980:119

142.　Declan Donnellan in BERRY, 1989:194

143.　Patrick Marber in EYRE, 2009:284

144.　ALFREDS, 2007:205

145.　William H. Macy in LUCKHURST & VELTMAN, 2001:65

146.　BARBA, 1991

147.　Simon Russell Beale in LEIPACHER, 2011:28

148.　Sam Mendes in LEIPACHER, 2011:23

149.　Linda Marlowe in LUCKHURST & VELTMAN, 2001:81

150.　LECOQ, 2002:92

151.　WALTER, 2003:122

152.　*Ibid.*

153.　NEWLOVE, 1993:12

154.　GRAHAM & HOGGETT, 2008:36

155.　Jane Hartley, unpublished interview with the author, 4/07/11

156.　SMILEY, 2005:147

157.　WALTER, 2003:185

158. *Ibid.*:37

159. SMILEY, 2005:172

160. John Willett quoting Brecht's *Short Organum on Theatre*, 1964:197

161. AYCKBOURN, 2002:148

162. LECOQ, 2000:76

163. DONNELLAN, 2002:171

164. WRIGHT, 2006:62

165. SMILEY, 2005:173

166. Judi Dench in EYRE, 2009:59

167. GOOCH, 2001:72

Section 5: Workshopping Scenes

168. Declan Donnellan in BERRY, 1989:192

169. EDGAR, 2009:201

170. MAMET, 1998:76

171. WATERS, 2010:13

172. Sam Mendes in LEIPACHER, 2011:21

173. WALTER, 2003:42

174. ALFREDS, 2007:348

175. John Berger in COMPLICITE, 2010:77

176. COMPLICITE, 2010:56

177. The following three tracks have worked well for this exercise: John Adams' 'The Chairman Dances', from *Nixon in China*; Dave Brubeck's 'Take Five'; Stereophonics' 'Jots and Loops Track 1'.

178. GRAHAM & HOGGETT, 2009:46

179. Katie Mitchell in SHEVTSOVA & INNES, 2009:188

180. The exercises in *Through the Body* are called Rhythm-scapes 1 and 2 p. 123–127

181. BRECHT, 1980:115

182. MAMET, 1998:76

183. STANISLAVSKY, 1936:142

184. LECOQ, 2000:36

185. Declan Donnellan quoted in READE, 1991:110

186. MAMET, 1998:62

187. John McGrath in EYRE, 2009:268

188. Peter Brook in EYRE, 2009:20

189. Peter Hall in EYRE, 2009:44

190. Robert Lepage in INNES, 2009:135

191. AYCKBOURN, 2002:149

192. *Ibid.*:38

193. GRAHAM & HOGGETT, 2009:129

194. *Ibid.*:50. And they state that 'these include principles of editing, how images are framed, how to control the focus of the viewer, the use of music to soundtrack a story, how scenes are ordered and their interrelation, the specificity of filmic narrative and the implications of a specific colour palette.'

195. *Ibid.*:55

196. *Ibid.*:68

197. Jane Hartley, unpublished interview with the author, 4/07/11

198. AYCKBOURN, 2002:145

199. *Daily Telegraph* review of *On the Waterfront*

200. Alain Gautre in LECOQ, 2006:136

201. Annabel Arden in MANFULL, 1999:124

202. Steven Berkoff in EYRE, 2009:290

203. Declan Donnellan in GIANNACHI & LUCKHURST, 1999:22–3

204. Simon Bolitho: Edvard Munch Exhibition leaflet, Tate Modern, 2012, Room 5.

205. 'Impressionists rather than surrealists, [using] a variety of colours and textures to elicit an almost emotional response from the viewer but always guiding the viewer towards an understanding of what is being presented' GRAHAM & HOGGETT, 2009:129

Section 6: Inside the Words

206. WALTER, 2003:155

207. BARBA, 2010:40

208. LECOQ, 2000:137

209. CALLOW, 1985:93-4

210. LECOQ, 2000:137

211. DONNELLAN, 2002:157

212. Declan Donnellan quoted in READE, 1991:110

213. AYCKBOURN, 2002:93

214. HARROP, 1992:98

215. BROOK, 1993:75

216. BERRY, 2008:1

217. Linda Marlowe in LUCKHURST & VELTMAN, 2001:83

218. BERRY, 2008:4

219. *Ibid.*

220. Annabel Arden in LUCKHURST & VELTMAN, 2001:7

221. GASKILL, 2010:84

222. DONNELLAN, 2002:269

223. *Ibid.*:245

224. McBURNEY, 2009:169

225. Judi Dench in EYRE, 2009:60

226. DONNELLAN, 2002:257

227. Stephen Fry 'First Person: In the library I discovered that being gay was a blessing' in *The Times Saturday Review*, 28th January 2012, p. 6

228. Annabel Arden in MANFULL, 1999:122

229. BERRY, 2001:62

230. LECOQ, 2006:91

231. GASKILL, 2010:57

232. DONNELLAN, 2002:67

233. GOOCH, 2001:41

234. LECOQ, 2006:92

235. GASKILL, 1998:89

236. WATERS, 2010:130

237. Kathryn Hunter in TUSHINGHAM, 1995:72

238. GASKILL, 2010:56

239. David Hare in *Platform Papers 8: Playwrights*, Royal National Theatre, 1993:6

240. WATERS, 2010:116

241. BERRY, 2001:126

Section 7: Around the Words

242. Sarah Kane in SAUNDERS, 2002:50

243. GASKILL, 1998:111

244. Peter Hall, quoted by BRADBY, 2001:1

245. Simon McBurney in '*Endgame* Education Pack', p. 5

246. Beckett quoted in COHN, 1980:231

247. 'Mime played a more important part in Beckett's theatre than most critics have been willing to acknowledge.' KNOWLSON, 2003:122

248. HALL, 2000:23

249. BRECHT, 1980:106

250. George Steiner in *The Death of Tragedy* quoted by BARBA, 1991:234

251. GASKILL, 2010:8

252. BOGART, 2001:68

253. GRAHAM & HOGGETT, 2009:131

254. William H. Macy in LUCKHURST & VELTMAN, 2001:62

255. GRAHAM & HOGGETT, 2009:83

256. *Ibid.*:170

257. Simon McBurney in SHEVTSOVA & INNES, 2009:170

258. Ariane Mnouchkine in LECOQ, 2006:131

259. Ronald Gray (1961:66) quoted in LEITER, 1991:170

260. BOND, 2009:xlv

261. Edward Bond interview, BBC Radio 3 *Nightwaves*, 19/10/11

262. Simon Kane quoted by IBALL, 2008:161

263. GOOCH, 2001:31

264. HARROP, 1992:61

265. Simon McBurney in GIANNACHI & LUCKHURST, 1999:77

266. Sarah Kane in SAUNDERS, 2002:42

267. Simon McBurney in COMPLICITE, 2010:99

268. WALTER, 2003:152

269. Annabel Arden in MANFULL, 1999:40

270. DONNELLAN, 2002:140

271. BERKOFF, 1989:203

272. Declan Donnellan in READE, 1991:24

273. WATERS, 2010:59

274. HARROP, 1992:40

275. LECOQ, 2006:70

276. Beckett in KNOWLSON, 2003:145

277 Peter Brook in *Platform Papers 6: Peter Brook*, Royal National
     Theatre, 1994:30

278. *Ibid.*

Section 8: Spacing and Pacing

279. Annabel Arden in LUCKHURST & VELTMAN, 2001:2

280. BROOK, 1998:131

281. CALLOW, 1985:192

282. Meyerhold in GLADHOV, 1997:115

283. LECOQ, 2006:53

284. *Ibid.*

285. The track they played was Imogen Heap's *Hide and Seek*. GRAHAM
     & HOGGETT, 2009:49

286. *Ibid.*:27–28

287. *Ibid.*:45

288. BERKOFF, 1978:8

289. *Ibid.*

290. BERKOFF, 1989:178

291. GRAHAM & HOGGETT, 2009:47

292. BRECHT, 1980:97

293. LECOQ, 2006:92

294. BARRAULT, 1974:169

295. Joan Littlewood in LEACH, 2006:40

296. WRIGHT, 2006:122

297. LECOQ, 2006:90

298. WRIGHT, 2006:105

299. BRECHT 1980:139

300. WRIGHT, 2006:114

301. WATERS, 2010:80

302. ALFREDS, 2007:279

303. BRECHT, trans. Willett, 1965:94

304. *Ibid.*

305. Abigail Rokison interview (2009): David Tennant on Hamlet, Shakespeare, 5:3, 292-304, DOI:10.1080/17450910903138062, date accessed 14/07/2013

306. CALLOW, 1985:188

307. BRECHT, 1980:102

308. GRAHAM & HOGGETT, 2009:23

309. Michael Sheen in LUCKHURST & VELTMAN, 2001:120

310. Macdonald commented in an interview: 'The rain between scenes may have come partly from looking at photographs of Bosnia at the time, because... much of the play is rooted in that conflict', in SAUNDERS, 2009:156

311. Robert Lepage in SHEVTSOVA & INNES, 2009:135

312. LECOQ, 2006:88

Afterword

313. BROOK, 1993:14

314. For further reading relating to these new developments, Bruce McConachie's *Theatre and Mind* in the Palgrave Macmillan series (2013) is recommended.

315. Nancy Meckler in MANFULL, 1999:70

316. Katie Mitchell in MANFULL, 1999:74–75

317. Simon McBurney in COMPLICITE, 2010:9

Index of Games

Index of Names and Titles

Index of Ideas and Concepts

www.nickhernbooks.co.uk

facebook.com/nickhernbooks

twitter.com/nickhernbooks